HISTORIC PROTESTANTISM
AND PREDESTINATION

HISTORIC

PROTESTANTISM

AND

PREDESTINATION

by

Harry Buis

Presbyterian and Reformed Publishing Company
Philadelphia, Pennsylvania

LIBRARY OF CONGRESS CATALOGUE CARD NUMBER 58-59920

Printed in the United States of America

To

The Vriesland Reformed Church of Zeeland, Michigan
whose people love the whole counsel of God.

TABLE OF CONTENTS

INTRODUCTION

The doctrine of predestination and the doctrines associated with it under the term "Calvinism" have for centuries been the source of bitter controversies within the Church. Our purpose in considering this subject is certainly not to arouse further controversy. In fact, we seek to write in an irenic rather than in a polemic spirit. On the other hand, we are convinced that the Calvinistic doctrine of predestination is Biblical; and therefore ought not to be avoided, but rather, as with all Biblical doctrines, should be understood and proclaimed. We are convinced that the bitterness of this controversy has been due in part to misunderstandings; therefore our emphasis in this book is not so much to present our opinions, as it is to bring to light the facts which we have discovered in our research, facts relating to what Christians have believed down through the centuries concerning this subject, and the reason why they have held these beliefs. Our hope is that the presentation of these facts will be of some value in helping those with divergent views on the subject come to a clearer understanding of the truth.

All of us need more light on this difficult subject, and we hope that many of all denominations will profit from this work. However, we write particularly to help people within the Reformed and Presbyterian Churches, both ministers and laymen, who feel somewhat apologetic about the fact that the creeds of their churches teach predestination. Many within these circles are not fully convinced concerning their churches' teachings on this doctrine. We hope that the Biblical and historical perspective provided by this book will produce stronger convictions in the hearts of such people. We believe such convictions should overwhelm the believer with the marvel of God's grace, and thus produce a greater measure of those qualities so vital to the Christian life, namely humility and gratitude. To God be the glory.

Harry Buis

HISTORIC PROTESTANTISM AND PREDESTINATION

Chapter One

THE COMMON FALLACY

Many laymen, and some theologians as well, assume that the doctrine of predestination and the doctrines associated with it are the product of the supposedly gloomy mind of John Calvin. Those who have really studied the works of Calvin come to far different conclusions, they are thrilled by the warmth of godly devotion of this great Bible scholar. But, be that as it may, Calvin, contrary to popular opinion, was certainly not the creator of the doctrine of predestination. Yet even such a fine historian as Will Durant in his recent book *The Reformation* severely criticizes Calvin because he assumes this to be so.

The fact is that the doctrine of predestination was introduced into the main stream of the theology of the Christian Church by Augustine *more than one thousand years before the days of John Calvin.* Interest in this doctrine was later revived, not by Calvin, but by the Reformers who lived before the days of the Great Reformation, namely, Wycliffe and Huss. Furthermore, the doctrine of predestination was strongly affirmed by all of Calvin's fellow Reformers, those who immediately preceded him, as well as those who

1

followed him, with but one notable exception, Melanchthon, who at first shared this conviction, but who later repudiated it.

Our purpose in this book is to seek to document the above statements with the greatest care, especially concentrating on the demonstration of the fact that Martin Luther held as strong a doctrine of predestination as did John Calvin. This last fact is of special importance, since Luther played such a key role in the birth of Protestantism and since he was the father of such a great branch of the Protestant Church, a branch which now largely repudiates the doctrine of predestination which he taught so emphatically. In passing, Calvin's own concept of predestination will be considered in order to note that if wasn't nearly as one-sided as many of his critics affirm. We shall then investigate the reasons for the fact that this cardinal Reformation doctrine lost ground in so many areas of the Protestant Church. Then we shall investigate the biblical basis for the doctrine, since this was the great reason for its acceptance by the Reformers. Finally we shall conclude by trying to give some helpful explanations of the doctrine of predestination, which we hope will help make it more understandable to the modern mind.

Before we develop the above theses, we wish to show that our fundamental position, that the other Reformers and especially Martin Luther held to the doctrine of predestination as strongly as did Calvin, is not a novel idea of our own creation. This fact has been accepted by many theologians, *but* this significant truth has not been sufficiently communicated to the Church at large. To demonstrate that our position is not a theological novelty, at this point we shall quote the opinions of a number of theologians:

G. P. Fisher, famous church historian from Yale, said, speaking of predestination, "This doctrine, at the outset, indeed, was common to all the Reformers. Predestination is asserted by Luther in his book on the 'Servitude of the

2

Will,' even in relation to wickedness, *in terms more emphatic than the most extreme statements of Calvin*. Melanchthon, for a considerable period, wrote in the same strain. Zwingli, in his metaphysical theory, did not differ from his brother Reformers. They were united in reviving the Augustinian theology, in opposition to the Pelagian doctrine, which affected in a greater or less degree all the schools of Catholic theology."[1] (Italics in this and the following quotations are mine—H.B.)

Neander, the German church historian, speaking of Zwingli's position, said, "It is therefore erroneous that the harshest and most logical form of this doctrine was derived from Calvin."[2] Of Calvin, he said, "In reference to this controversy, *nothing new proceeded from him;* he only maintained against the reactions, the earlier doctrine of absolute Predestination."[3]

E. F. Karl Mueller of the University of Erlangen said, "In the early days of Protestantism, predestination, as the expression of the power of grace from personal experience, opposed individual certainty of salvation to the claims of the Church, and formed *the one central dogma common to all the Reformers.*"[4]

Babingthen said, "The term Calvinism has been widely applied to the religious system which sets the doctrine of Predestination in the forefront of its teaching. Those who use this term ignore or overlook the fact that the doctrine, so far from being peculiar to Calvin, is *common to all the leading Reformers*. But what is still more persistently ignored or over ooked is the fact that the doctrine in the form which it a sumed in the theology of the Reformation, originated with the greatest Father of the Western Church, St. Au-

---

[1] G. P. Fisher, *The Reformation*, p. 200.
[2] Neander, *Lectures on the History of Christian Dogmas*, p. 668.
[3] *Ibid.*, p. 673.
[4] E. F. Karl Mueller, "Predestination" in *The New Schaff-Herzog Encyclopedia of Religious Knowledge*, Vol. IX, p. 196.

3

gustine, and that the foundation on which Calvin rested his defense of the doctrine is as purely scriptural as St. Augustine."[5]

Benjamin B. Warfield, the great Princeton theologian, said, "It is a truth deserving the strongest emphasis that the system of doctrine which Calvin taught, and by his powerful commendation of which his greatest work for the world was wrought, *was not peculiar to himself, was in no sense new*—was, in point of fact, just 'the Gospel' common to him and all the Reformers, on the ground of which they spoke of themselves as 'Evangelicals,' and by the recovery of which was wrought out the revolution which we call the Reformation. Calvin did not originate this system of truth; as 'a man of the second generation' he inherited it. . . .

"The system of doctrine taught by Calvin is just the Augustinianism common to the whole body of the Reformers —for the Reformation was, as from the spiritual point of view a great revival of religion, so from the theological point of view a great revival of Augustinianism. And this Augustinianism is taught by him not as an independent discovery of his own, but fundamentally as *he learned it from Luther*, whose fertile conceptions he completely assimilated, and most directly and in much detail from Martin Bucer."[6]

Louis Berkhof,[7] Herman Bavinck,[8] and A. M. Hunter[9] to name just a few other theologians, all speak in similiar terms. Hence we see that many theologians have recognized this important truth of which the Church at large is almost completely ignorant: The doctrine of predestination was a cardinal doctrine held in common by all of the Reformers; and was therefore originally one of the fundamentals of Protestantism. Those, therefore, who hold this truth today

[5] J. H. Babingthen, *The Reformation*, p. 84.
[6] B. B. Warfield, *Calvin and Augustine*, p. 22.
[7] L. Berkhof, *The History of Christian Doctrines*, p. 153.
[8] H. Bavinck, *The Doctrine of God*, p. 353.
[9] A. M. Hunter, *The Teaching of Calvin*, p. 96.

4

ought not to apologize for their position; for they accept the historic Protestantism which those who reject the doctrine deny.

Chapter Two

THE COMMON HERITAGE

Both Calvin and Luther were deeply influenced by the theological and philosophical thinking which took place in the centuries preceding them. They were scholars acquainted with the writings of previous ages. They, like ourselves, were recipients of a theological inheritance. They rebelled against the errors of their age not with theological novelty but by a return, largely through Augustine, to the Scriptures. At this point, the question is: What were the highlights of the history of theological thought with regard to the subject of predestination and free will in the centuries from New Testament days to the Reformation?

The Early Church Fathers

Honesty requires us to recognize that the early Fathers did not deal with predestination, but rather stressed the freedom of the will. The thinking of the Fathers prior to Augustine was largely shaped by their opposition to the Gnostic heresy. The Gnostics proudly thought that they alone were initiated into the mysteries of true knowledge.

They sought to combine Christian and non-Christian thought even as do the cults today. One of the common features of Gnosticism was a dualism between the God of creation and the God of the New Testament. Involved in this idea was an emphasis on the physical necessity of evil and a consequent denial of the freedom of the will. This was part of a larger Greek emphasis on blind Fate. It was therefore in reaction to this heresy that the Fathers emphasized the freedom of the will and stressed the idea that sin did not destroy but only weakened the original powers with which man was created. Yet, even before Augustine, an increasing tendency to recognize the work of God's grace can be traced in the thinking of the Church Fathers.

The Alexandrian school emphasized free will most strongly. Clement of Alexandria said that to believe or to disbelieve is as much at the command of our will as to philosophize or not to philosophize. He recognized a work of God in the soul, but his emphasis was on the idea that the sinner must take the initiative. Origen's view coincided with that of Clement. Origen said, "But in fact foreknowledge *precedes* foreordination. . . . God observed beforehand the sequence of future events, and noticed the inclination of some men towards piety, on their own responsibility, and their stirrings towards piety which followed on this inclination; he sees how they devote themselves to living a virtuous life, and he foreknew them, knowing the present, and foreknowing the future. . . . And if anyone in reply asks whether it is possible for the events which God foreknew not to happen, we shall answer, Yes, and there is no necessity determining this happening or not happening."[1] Origen considers the subject of human responsibility and predestination at length in *De Principiis III* where he discusses various Scripture passages which seem to teach predestination. In each case he seeks to show that the passage in no

[1] Origen, *Comm. In Ep. ad Romanos*, i.

7

way lessens human responsibility, but only teaches that we need God's help, so that the result is a matter of cooperation between God and man.

The later Alexandrian school also emphasized free will, yet not as strongly as its predecessors. Those of this school included Athanasius, Basil, Gregory Nazianzen, Gregory Nyssa, Cyril of Jerulsalem, and Cyril of Alexandria.

The school of Antioch, including Theodore of Mopsuestia, Chrysostom, and Theodoret had an anthropology similar to the later Alexandrian scholars. Amongst them, however, existed an increased recognition of the influence of the sin of Adam on the whole race. The position of these two schools is what is commonly called synergism; that is, the belief that regeneration is the cooperative work of the human will and of the Holy Spirit.

In the Western or Latin Church, Tertullian introduced traducianism, which is the theory that the soul of the individual is propagated along with the body by human generation. This concept prepared the way for a greater recognition of the power of innate sin. Tertullian's position on the relation of free will to grace, however, was still practically the same as the synergism of the Eastern Church. Yet he placed less emphasis on human power and more on the work of God. Cyprian moved a little further in this same direction. The position of Ambrose and Hilary placed still greater emphasis on the grace of God, but it was still synergistic. Ambrose, who holds a place of strategic importance because of his influence on Augustine, said: "God calls those whom he deigns to call; he makes him pious whom he wills to make pious, for if he had willed he could haved changed the impious into pious."[2] "He who follows Christ, if asked why he was willing to be in Christ, must confirm because it so pleased himself, but in saying that,

[2] Ambrose, *In. Luc.*, 7, 27.

8

he does not deny that it so pleased God."[3]   On the other hand, Ambrose also said: "The apostle says, 'Whom he foreknew, them he also predestinated': for he did not predestinate before he foreknew, but to those whose merit he foreknew, he predestinated the rewards of merit."[4]   In other words, he, like Origen, based predestination on God's foreknowledge of man's merit, which in reality leaves the initiative with man rather than with God.   Ambrose, then, was still far from the position later taken by Augustine, yet he had moved a considerable distance from the position of the earliest Fathers.

Augustine

When Augustine came upon the scene the entire situation was changed.   He taught absolute predestination, and his influential position in the Church brought the subject into the center of theological thought.   Absolute predestination was not Augustine's original position.   His original position was synergistic like that of his predecessors.   He held this position for two reasons: first, he had been nurtured in the theology of Ambrose, and second, he was in the early period of his Christian life engaged in controversy with the Manicheans who had the same doctrine of sin as a natural necessity which the Gnostics had held in the preceding period.   In this first phase of his thinking, Augustine made such statements as the following: "It belongs to us to believe and to will, but to Him to give to those that believe and will the power to do well, through the Holy Spirit, through whom love is shed abroad in our hearts,"[5] and "God has not predestinated any one except whom He foreknew would believe and answer his call."[6]   Many years later, speaking of his

[3] *Ibid.*, 1, 10.

[4] Ambrose, *De fide*, lib. V. n. 83.

[5] Augustine, *Exposito quarumdam propositionum ex Epistola ad Romanos*, 61.

[6] *Ibid.*, 55.

9

views at this earlier period, he said that he "had not yet very carefully inquired into or sought out the nature of the election of grace of which the apostle speaks."[7] Augustine is referring here to what Paul says in Romans 10:1-5.

Shortly after Augustine was ordained to the office of bishop in 395, he changed his position from synergism to monergism (literally, one work), that is, regeneration is the work of the Holy Spirit alone. According to his own testimony, one verse of Scripture was primarily responsible for producing this change: "For who maketh thee to differ from another? and what hast thou that thou didst not receive: now if thou didst receive it, why dost thou glory, as if thou hadst not received it?" (I Cor. 4:7). Speaking of Semi-Pelagians, Augustine said, "It was especially by this passage that I myself also was convinced, when I erred in a similar manner thinking that the faith by which we believe in God is not the gift of God, but that it is in us of ourselves, and that by it we obtain the gifts of God whereby we may live temperately and righteously and piously in this world. For I did not think that faith was preceded by God's grace—so that by it means might be given us what we might profitably ask—except in the sense that we could not believe unless the proclamation of the truth preceded; but to consent after the Gospel had been preached to us, I thought belonged to ourselves, and came to us from ourselves."[8]

Commenting on this same verse, he said in another of his writings: "How can it be explained that the Gospel reaches one man and not another? and that even the same dispensations act quite differently on different persons? It belongs to God to furnish the means which lead every man to believe —consequently the reason of the difference can only be, that according to his own decree, it seems good to withhold it from one and not from another. All men, in consequence of

[7] Augustine, *De praedestinatione sanctorum*, 3, 7.
[8] *Ibid.*, 3, 7.

the first transgression, are exposed to perdition; in this state there can be no higher movement, therefore, none at all, in them towards conversion. But God out of compassion chooses some to whom he imparts divine grace (*gratia efficax*), which operates upon them, in an irresistible manner, but yet in accordance with their rational nature, so that they cannot do otherwise than follow it. The rest he leaves to their merited perdition."[9]

The preceding quotations from Augustine clearly demonstrate the fact that the teaching of the Scriptures, and especially the writings of the Apostle Paul, were responsible for leading Augustine to his position on predestination. No doubt his reflections upon his own previous struggle with sin, in which he had found himself so utterly helpless, enabled him to appreciate these Scriptural teachings far more than they can be appreciated by people who have never experienced such a vigorous struggle with the power of sin.

Were there any other factors involved in leading Augustine to espouse absolute predestination? Harnack believes that the influence of Caius Marius Victorinus, who wrote commentaries on the Pauline epistles, was another factor. He says, "Unless all signs deceive, Augustine received from Victorinus the impulse which led him to assimilate Paul's type of religious thought."[10] Harnack also says, "The most interesting features, because the most important for Augustine are: (1) that Victorinus gives strong expression to the doctrine of predestination—only he feels compelled in opposition to Manichaenism to maintain the freedom of the will; and (2) that, especially in his commentaries, he places the highest value on *justification by faith alone* in opposition to all moralism."[11] Not enough evidence is available to ascertain how great an influence Victorinus actually had on Au-

[9] Augustine, *Lib. i. quaestio.* 2.
[10] Harnack, *History of Dogma*, p. 34.
[11] *Ibid.*, p. 36.

gustine at this point. Augustine's references to his acquaintance with the life and works of Victorinus in his *Confessions* prove that there was at least some influence.

As has already been mentioned, it was at about the time of his ordination to the office of bishop that Augustine's new view became clarified, so that in his first writing after his consecration, the *De diversis quaestionibus ad Simplicianum* (396 or 397 A.D.) he clearly stated his new view. It was not until many years later that Augustine's controversy with Pelagius began, so that Augustine's view can in no way be considered as a reaction against Pelagius.

Augustine wrote so many volumes on the subject that it would be beyond the scope of this work to consider each of them in detail. The following quotations, however, will give some idea of Augustine's position: "It cannot, therefore, be doubted that human wills are not able to resist the will of God, so that he may not do what he will."[12] "The predestination of God, which is in the good man, is a preparation . . . for grace, but grace is the effect of this predestination."[13] "Therefore whoever have in the most provident ordering of God been foreknown, predestined, called, justified, and glorified, although yet, I will not say unregenerated but even yet unborn, are now the sons of God and can by no means perish."[14] "The elect are not elected because they believe, but they are elected that they may believe."[15]

Augustine evidently took the infralapsarian position (i.e., that God did not decree the fall) for he speaks of God foreknowing the fall of Adam, but not compelling it.[16] Augustine, however, did teach double predestination, that is, that God ordained the damnation of the lost as well as the

---

[12] Augustine, *De Correptione et gratia*, 14. 45. *sanctorum*, viii, 16: xvii. 34.
[13] Augustine, *Praedest*. 10. 19; *don. perev*. 9. 21.
[14] Augustine, *De Correptione et gratia*, 9. 23.
[15] Augustine, *De Praedestinatione*
[16] Augustine, *De correptione et gratia*, 12. 37.

salvation of those who are saved. He speaks of "A pre-destination unto eternal death,"[17] and of "those who were predestined unto everlasting destruction."[18] Yet he maintained that God does not foreordain unto damnation in the same sense that he foreordains unto salvation.

Thus it was that Augustine, more than ten centuries before Calvin, introduced the teaching of predestination as a cardinal doctrine of the Christian faith. Augustine taught the doctrine in practically the exact form in which Calvin later taught it, and he certainly emphasized it at least as much as Calvin did. Augustine's teaching, however, did not go unchallenged for long, and the principal challenger was Pelagius.

Pelagius was a British monk, a man of blameless character, who was simply unable to grasp the depth of the struggle against sin which Augustine had experienced. His concept of monkish morality caused him to believe that it is possible to do more than the law of God requires. When he visited Rome in 400 A.D., he was deeply disturbed by the immorality which was so prevalent there. He was furthermore shocked by the position of Augustine as expressed in the prayer in his *Confessions*, "Give what thou commandest and command what thou wilt." He encountered people whose incorrect application of the Augustinian concept of grace had led them to spiritual negligence, people who claimed to be believers but who did not live the Christian life; and as a result of these experiences, Pelagius began to combat this conception of grace. He believed that originally Adam was morally neutral, and that the only difference between us and Adam is the fact that we have bad examples before us which tend to lead us in the wrong direction. Since, in his view, there is actually no such reality as original sin, in turning from evil man is not dependent on the grace of God. Pelagius thus went

[17] Augustine, *De. an. et ejus orig.* IV, 10: *De civ.* XXII, 24.
[18] Augustine, *John Ev. Tract.* 48.

13

beyond the early church in the opposite direction from that in which Augustine had moved.

The controversy which resulted from Pelagius' position began when Caelestius, a friend of Pelagius, was accused of heresy by Paulinus who was an advocate of Augustine's teachings. Caelestius was excommunicated as a result. Pelagius was then charged with heresy, but his defence satisfied the authorities in the Eastern branch of the Church, and as a result, the charge was dropped. As a consequence of this action, Jerome attacked the Eastern Church fiercely, and Augustine also opposed but with greater moderation. At Rome in 416-418 A.D., the Roman bishop Zozimus at first cleared Pelagius, and then, after a strong protest was registered by the council at Carthage, he reversed his decision. Finally, at the ecumenical council of Ephesus in 431 A.D., Pelagianism was condemned.

Post-Augustinian Developments

The result of the official condemnation of Pelagianism, however, did not mean that pure Augustinianism came to dominate the thought of the Church; but in reality it was a form of Semi-Pelagianism which became the accepted doctrine of Roman Catholicism and it was against this Semi-Pelagianism that Luther and Calvin later fought. This Semi-Pelagianism was in reality a return to a synergistic position.

Following the condemnation of Pelagianism, there was considerable controversy between Augustinians and semi-Pelagians. Except for absolute predestination, the semi-Pelagians accepted many of Augustine's doctrines so that some scholars prefer to label them semi-Augustinians, but this is a mistake since predestination is the crucial point which divides the two views. Augustine having died in 430 A.D., the leading advocates of Augustinianism were

14

Prosper of Aquaitanis who wrote *Liber Contra Collatorem* and *Carmen de Ingratis* in which he characterized semi-Pelgianism as an impossible fence-straddling position; the unknown author of *De Vocatione Gentium* who attempted to maintain the Augustinian position while seeking to avoid the features of that position against which many people objected; and another anonymous writer who attempted to do the same thing in *Hypomnesticon*. Some of the other followers of Augustine further complicated the situation by taking a more extreme position than Augustine himself had taken.

The chief advocates of semi-Pelagianism were Cassian of Massilia (Marseilles) and Faustus the Bishop of Rhegium. While Faustus condemned Pelagius, he himself went beyond Cassian to a basically Pelagian position. Other advocates of Semi-Pelagianism were the anonymous author who satirized Augustinianism in *Praedestinatus,* and Vincent of Lerins. Vincent believed that the test of orthodoxy was that which has been believed "always, everywhere and by all." Applying this criterion, he claimed that Augustine's position was outside of the realm of Catholic doctrine, and therefore should be rejected.

Further controversy continued when the Scythian monks of Constantinople opposed Augustinianism, which was in turn defended by Fulgentius of Ruspe. The matter was considered at the Synod of Orange in 529 A.D., which resulted in a defeat for Semi-Pelagianism. This synod spoke in strong terms of the inability of man and the necessity of grace, yet it failed to take a stand in favor of absolute predestination and irresistible grace. It also rejected the doctrine of predestination to perdition, that is, double predestination. Pope Boniface II approved the statement of the Synod of Orange. Gregory the Great, elected Pope in 560 A.D., was an advocate of Augustinianism, but in reality his was a very much weakened form of that position. The growth of sacramentarianism further complicated the picture.

The Synod of Orange brought the controversy to a close until the ninth century when it was again renewed. At that time, Gottschalk, who had found peace for his own soul in Augustine's doctrine of election, aroused considerable animosity by contending for a double predestination which he applied on an equal basis to both the saved and the lost. Gottschalk's doctrine was condemned by Mayence in 848 A.D. In further debate, Prudentius, Ratramnus and Remigius defended double predestination. The opposing side was taken by Rabanus and Hincmar of Rheims.

The most interesting figure in the controversy which took place at this time was Johannes Scotus Erigena (not to be confused with Johannes Duns Scotus) who was called into the controversy by Hincmar to take his side, but who was actually too independent a thinker to take either side. Between 849 and 853 A.D., he wrote *De divina Praedestinatione,* in which he charged Gottschalk with heresy. His philosophical ideas led him to reject double predestination because he believed in the non-entity of sin and punishment. He developed several interesting points, however. One was with regard to the relationship of predestination and foreknowledge. Many opponents of predestination base predestination on God's foreknowledge of man's merit. We have noted that this was the position of Origen, and as we continue our examination of the history of the doctrine, we shall see that this idea reappears again and again. Those who take this position say that God predestinates people because He knows that they are going to believe or because He knows that they will merit salvation. This in reality makes predestination meaningless, for it bases salvation on merit rather than on grace. Erigena, however, pointed out that from God's standpoint there can be neither past nor future; for, since He is eternal, He sees all of us and He sees us all at

16

once. He declared that distinguishing between foreknowledge and foreordination is setting up a false antithesis, since God can know only what He does.

Another contribution which Erigena made was by way of an illustration which he used. He said that a man in the thickest darkness still retains the power of seeing, but doesn't really see until the light comes to him from some outside source. Likewise, according to Erigena, the will of man always retains the power of being good, though corrupted by original sin and his own actual sins and thus surrounded by darkness, so that he cannot attain to the exercise of this power until the light of grace cures the infirm will. There is a certain acuteness in this illustration, as it makes all of salvation dependent on God's grace which must first work, yet it maintains that the human will is a reality. Basically, however, Erigena was a universalist. His statement caused further controversy and his views were condemned by synods in 855 and in 859. The whole subject had in reality degenerated into an argument over words. The Councils of Chiersy and of Valence both met in 853 and considered the problem. The decision of Chiersy opposed double predestination, while that of Valence was in favor of it. At Savonieres and Langres in 859, and at Toucy in 860 the subject was discussed further, and attempts were made at compromise solutions.

Pre-Reformation Thought

In the intervening centuries prior to the Reformation, several great theologians stand out as advocates of Augustinian thought. Anselm (1033-1109 A.D.), the English theologian who is famous for his satisfaction theory of the atonement, was one of them. Anselm's major contribution was his clarification of the definition of freedom of the will. In his *De libero arbitrio,* he insisted that the common definition of freedom as the power of sinning or of not sinning is totally inadequate. The man who can only do right is really more free than the one who can do wrong. To prove this point, Anselm quoted the saying of Jesus that he who sins is the slave of sin. Anselm distinguished between true freedom and what he calls the voluntary faculty. Fallen man does not possess true freedom although he does retain the voluntary faculty. Anselm's doctrine of original sin followed that of Augustine. Anselm also wrote *De concordia praedcientiae praedestinationis cum libero arbitrio* in which he championed the Augustinian position.

Peter Lombard (c.1105-c.1160 A.D.), famous for his *Sentences,* took a similar stand. According to Lombard, there is no merit antecedent to grace. With regard to the relationship of God's foreknowledge to actual events, neither is the actual ground of the other, but each is to the other a *causa sine qua non.* As a result of his sacramentarianism, however, Lombard beclouded his concept of grace, by insisting that baptism and penance are necessary supplements to the work of Christ.

Thomas Aquinas (c. 1225-1274 A.D.), by far the outstanding theologian of the Middle Ages, was definitely Augustinian.[19] As Harnack says, "How entirely dependent Thomas is upon Augustine is shown by the doctrine of predestination, which he has taken over in all its strictness."[20] Harnack also mentions that one of the characteristics of Thomas' *Summa* is its strict adherence to Augustinianism especially in the doctrines of God, predestination, sin and grace.[21] A study of the *Summa* itself proves this to be true. Question 23 is entitled "Of Predestination," and in eight articles con-

[19] Several books, unfortunately not in English, compare Aquinas to Calvin. They are: AD. R. Polman, *Predestinations leer van Augustines, Thomas van Aquino en Calvijn* and Herbert Olsson, *Calvin och Reformationens Theologi.*
[20] Harnack, *Op. Cit.,* Vol. VI, p. 136.
[21] *Ibid.,* p. 156.

tains a lengthy discussion of the subject. In the first article, Thomas says, "It is fitting that God should predestine men. For all things are subject to His providence, as was shown above." In the third article, he even states: "God does reprobate some." "Thus as men are ordained to eternal life through the providence of God, it likewise is part of that providence to permit some to fall away from that end; this is called reprobation. . . ." "God loves all men and all creatures, inasmuch as He wishes them all some good; but He does not wish every good to them all. So far, therefore, as He does not wish this particular good—namely, eternal life—He is said to hate or reprobate them." "Reprobation differs in its causality from predestination." "Reprobation isn't the cause of what is in the present—namely, sin; but it is the cause of the abandonment of God." "Although anyone reprobated by God cannot acquire grace, nevertheless that he falls into this or that particular sin comes from the use of his free-will. Hence it is rightly imputed to him as guilt." In article four, Thomas says, "God wills all men to be saved by His antecedent will, which is to will not simply but relatively; and not by His consequent will, which is to will simply."

In Article 5, Thomas discusses the question, "Whether the Fore-Knowledge of Merits is the Cause of Predestination?" His answer to this question includes the following statements: "Nobody has been so insane as to say that merit is the cause of divine predestination as regards the act of the predestinator." "So others said that merits following the effect of predestination are the reason of predestination. . . . But these seem to have drawn a distinction between that which flows from grace, and that which flows from free will, as if the same thing cannot come from both. . . . Now there is no distinction between what flows from free will, and what is of predestination. . . . Thus we might say that God preordained to give glory on account of merit, and that

19

He preordained to give grace to merit glory." . . . "Thus, it is impossible that the whole of the effect of predestination in general should have any cause as coming from us; because whatsoever is in man disposing him towards salvation, is all included under the effect of predestination; even the preparation for grace." In Article 6, Thomas discusses the question, "Whether predestination is certain?" and he answers thus: "Predestination most certainly and infallibly takes effect; yet it does not impose any necessity." In Article 7, he discusses the question, "Whether the number of the predestined is certain?" which question he answers with a definite affirmative.

Aquinas deals with various aspects of the subject of predestination in some of his other writings as well as in the *Summa*. For example, in one instance, he writes, "For his eternity touches with its presence the whole suite of time and transcends it; so that we may regard God as knowing the passage of time in his eternity, as one seated on a high rock sees with one glance the wayfarers passing by." In another passage, he states: "We must understand that the divine will of which we speak is outside being, and that this latter is penetrated by it in its entirety, even down to all its divisions. But the possible and the necessary are divisions of being and they have their origin in the divine will." . . . "The necessary and the possible are distinctions belonging to being; hence it follows that it belongs to God, whose power it is which is the cause of being, to bestow necessity or possibility on what he makes according to his providence."

In his *Compendium Theologia*, Thomas states: "Whence it is clear that it is not against the freedom of the will, if God moves the will of man; just as it is not against nature that God acts in natural things; but all inclination, whether natural or free, is from God, both having effect according to the nature of the thing it belongs to; so God moves things in accordance with their free nature." In his *Contra Gentiles*,

Thomas points out that although free-will excludes the determination of the will, as well as violence, which proceed from some cause which acts on it externally, it does not exclude the influence of a higher cause from which proceed both its being and its operation. Thus the Divine causality, which is most efficacious, causes the will to will in accordance with its nature, that is, freely, and when the will wills the good, its power and that of the First Cause are all one; while when it falls away and wills evil, God eternally knows this, for by a permissive decree He eternally allows the will's defection. Thus both the act of willing and the mode of that act (which is freedom) proceed from God, and so are known by Him in His essence as determined by His decree.

From the above quotations, it is evident that Thomas was definitely Augustinian in his outlook. He made some very fine philosophical distinctions which are sometimes difficult to follow, but it is evident that he considered the sovereign act of God as the underlying cause of the salvation of each individual. Furthermore, he also spoke of reprobation, although he made a careful distinction between God's positive decree to elect to salvation, and the permissiveness of his decree with regard to reprobation. With Anselm, he did not consider free will to be the power of self determination; in fact, he considered it as one of the forms in which the Divine decrees are realized. On the other hand, Thomas' teaching on sacramentarianism and merit, in practice, undercut his teachings on God's grace, and left Roman Catholicism with a doctrine of work-righteousness.

Duns Scotus (1265-1308 A.D.) was the outstanding "Pelagian" of the Middle Ages. He used the term predestination in various senses, but his emphasis on the "merit of the fit" shifted the deciding factor back to God's foreknowledge of an individual's worthiness. He spoke of grace as a principle cooperating with the human will. From the time of Duns Scotus onward, the Roman Catholic conception of grace was superficial. The outstanding exceptions within the Church of this period were Bradwardine and Wycliffe.

The Thomist, Thomas Bradwardine, Archbishop of Canterbury (1290-1349 A.D.), spoke strongly against the prevailing Pelagianism of his day. He wrote a large volume called *De causa Dei contra Pelagium* in which he tried to show that the theology and the practices of the Church of his time were Pelagian. He said, "In the schools of the philosophers I rarely heard a word concerning grace, . . . but I continually heard that we are the masters of our own free actions." He also said, that while he studied in these schools, Romans 9:16[22] seemed to him to be wrong, but "afterward. . . . I came to see that the grace of God far preceded all good works both in time and in nature—by grace I mean the will of God." Bradwardine was thoroughly Augustinian. He recognized foreknowledge as essentially a facet of predestination, rather than a foreknowledge of man's merit which preceded predestination. He believed that the results of being predestined included the gift of grace and our perseverance in salvation to the end of our life.

At this point we consider the Waldenses because of their possible influence on John Wycliffe in the matter of predestination. The Waldenses emphasized Bible study and maintained evangelical doctrine long before the Reformation. Evidence indicates that at least some of them were predestinarians. One of their creeds states in its second article: "All that have been, or shall be saved, have been chosen of God before all worlds." The fourth article of the same creed says: "Whosoever holdeth free-will, denieth wholly the predestination of God."[23] Aeneas Sylvius, who

[22] So then it is not of him that willeth, nor of him that runneth but of God that sheweth mercy.

[23] See J. P. Perrin, *Hist. des Albigeois and . . . des Vaudois*, which is based on firsthand documents some of which are reproduced. Parts have been translated into English.

22

afterward became Pope Pius II, charged that the doctrine of Calvin and the Waldenses was the same.

John Wycliffe (c. 1325-1384 A.D.), who was influenced by Bradwardine and possibly by the Waldenses, provided the outstanding example of Augustinianism and opposed the prevailing Pelagianism of the Roman Catholic Church prior to the Reformation. In his *De Ecclesia* he identified the true church with the number of the elect. According to Wycliffe, no one who is rejected by God from eternity can be a member of the true church. No one can be a member of this church except by God's predestination. He emphasized the idea that faith is a gift of God's grace. Seeberg's conclusion is: "Wycliffe also exalts predestination to the central place of his theology."[24] Huss followed the theology of Wycliffe completely, and therefore he also held a similar predestinarian position. He also wrote a treatise, *De Ecclesia,* which was practically a translation of Wycliffe's book.

Several other lesser pre-Reformation figures also were predestinarians. For example, Johann Wessel of Holland (c. 1419-1489), also called Wessel Harmenss Gansfort or Goisevoyrdt, was Augustinian in his doctrine. Ullman entitles his book on Wessel, *Johannes Wessel ein voorganger van Luther.* Luther, in a letter to Rhodius said, "If I had read his works earlier my enemies might think that Luther had absorbed everything from Wessel, his spirit is so in accord with mine." Erasmus once said that Wessel taught all Luther did only less violently. Luther became acquainted with Wessel's writings in 1520, after he had come to his own conclusions with regard to predestination. In 1522 and 1523, Luther published Wessel's treatises under the title *Farrago uberrima.* The first treatise, entitled *Concerning the Sure and Benign Providence of God,* includes the following statements: ". . . not only are all things done in accordance with his will but indeed by the exercise of his will. Unless

[24] Seeberg, *The History of Doctrines,* Vol. II, p. 208.

he wills it, they can not be done, no matter how powerful may be the causes operating through nature. Other co-operating causes therefore are neither complete nor principal causes, but God rules as the entire, the chief cause of all things. . . . We may truly cooperate with God. And in this God makes us cooperate, because without him we can do nothing."[25]

In the second treatise, entitled *The Incarnation and Passion of Christ*, Wessel says: "he . . . cleanseth the heart of the faithful by faith; but not because of faith, but because of the speech and word of God which quickeneth a man." He further safeguards against the idea that faith is a work of man by which we are saved, a very common idea which actually provides a new form of work-righteousness, in several of his "Propositions concerning the Grace of God": Proposition 17: "Hence it is not our faith . . . that constitutes our righteousness; but it is the purpose of God," and Proposition 22: ". . . our justification (which nevertheless ultimately dependeth solely upon the purpose of God)." Others of the Brethren of the Common Life, for example, Johann Pupper of Goch, held similar sentiments.

The history of the doctrine generally associated with the name of Calvin has now been traced as it unfolded in the centuries prior to Luther's arrival upon the scene. We have seen that this doctrine was completely missing in the theology of the early Church Fathers, although the beginnings of some degree of appreciation for the sovereign nature of the grace of God appeared in the time immediately preceding that of Augustine. With the coming of Augustine, a strong emphasis was placed on sovereign grace and because of his great influence in the Church, this emphasis received serious consideration. However, we have also seen that from the time of Augustine onward a constant strug-

[25] See E. W. Miller, *Wessel Gansfort Life and Writings* which includes a translation of the *Farrago*.

24

gle took place between those who emphasized the preeminence of divine grace and those who emphasized the importance of human merit which the latter made the basis for any form of predestination which they were willing to consider. The result usually was that a compromising synergistic doctrine of cooperation between man and God was accepted. This, in reality, emptied the concept of grace of its true meaning. However, a few outstanding exceptions to this phenomenon have been noted. The practical result of the acceptance of synergism was that by the time Luther appeared on the scene, the emphasis of the Roman Catholic Church was on human merit and human works, rather than on salvation as a marvelous gift of God's grace.

To supplement our own analysis of this trend of doctrine, it will be of value to consider Harnack's summary of the situation in the centuries immediately preceding the Reformation:

"What has already been briefly hinted at above may be distinctly stated here—the problem was *the elimination of Augustinianism from the ecclesiatical doctrine.* . . . No doubt the Church had accepted Augustinianism, but with the secret reservation that it was to be molded by its own mode of thought. We have seen to what extent there was success in that in the period that ends, and in the period that begins, with Gregory the Great. Gottschalk already experienced what it costs in Catholicism to represent Augustinianism. . . .

"In the Pelagianism and Probabalism of Nominalism there lies the express apostasy from Augustinianism. But just because the apostasy was so manifest, there could not fail to be a certain reaction—though certainly no longer a strong one—in the Church. Not only did the Dominican Order, in their defending the theology of their great teacher, Thomas, persistently defend Augustine also (though, not, as a rule, in the most important points), but men also appeared in the fourteenth and fifteenth centuries who observed the *Pelagian* tendency of Nominalism, and strenuously resisted in the spirit of Augustine. Here Bradwardine must first be mentioned (ob. 1349) who places the *entire* Augustine, together with the predestinarian doctrine in strong opposition to the Pelagian tendency of the period. On him Wycliff was dependent as a theologian, and as Huss took all his theological thoughts from Wycliff, and introduced them into Bohemia and Germany, Bradwardine is really to be signalized as the theologian who gave the impulse to the Augustinian reactions that accompanied the history of the Church till the time of Staupitz and Luther, and that prepared the way for the Reformation."[26]

From the history of the doctrine which thus far has been outlined, several points of importance with regard to the thesis of our book present themselves. Our thesis, it will be recalled, is that predestination and the doctrines associated with it are not the invention of John Calvin but rather that he shared them with his fellow Reformers, and in fact, with men who lived centuries before him. In fact, the foregoing study of this history has made it clear that the grace versus merit problem was considered, and the predestinarian position accepted, by a number of significant men in the centuries prior to Calvin. We see furthermore that it was this background which set the stage for the coming of Martin Luther. We notice in particular that there are certain men whose names are outstanding in Church history because they grasped the fundamental concepts of the true gospel in the midst of a Church which had obscured this gospel by her teachings on work righteousness. These men, Augustine, Wycliffe, and Huss, to name the most outstanding ones, were the men who also followed consistently through with the concept of grace so that they also believed in predestination.

[26] Harnack, *Op. Cit.*, Vol. VI, p. 166-170.

Let those who are so quick to oppose the doctrine of pre-destination and to blacken the name of Calvin pause to realize that they thus oppose not simply Calvin but these heroes of the faith as well; let them pause to realize that by opposing this doctrine they place themselves on the side of the theologians of the Middle Ages who obliterated the concept of the grace of God and who taught that men are able to get to heaven by doing the good works which are commanded by the Roman Catholic Church. In the period prior to the Reformation, there were only two sides in this issue: the eminent few who preached a gospel later associated with Protestantism and who consistent with the gospel of grace also maintained the doctrine of predestination; and, on the other hand, those who held the Roman Catholic position and who taught that salvation was attainable through good works.

Chapter Three

LUTHER'S "ROMANS"

Turning to the writings of Luther himself, one finds a
considerable amount of material on the doctrine of predestination and on the associated doctrines. We shall seek
to present the most important excerpts from this material in
chronological order as much as possible, although there are
scholars who claim that there was really little change in
Luther's main ideas and therefore that it is not necessary
to be especially concerned with chronology. For example,
Kerr prefaces his valuable *Compend of Luther's Theology*
with the statement: "The position taken here, not without
good grounds, is that in the consideration of Luther's main
doctrinal contributions no importance attaches to change
and development since these, where ever they occur, are
not of a radical character."[2] Seeberg likewise says, "The
difference between the 'first form' and the later forms of
Luther's theology are commonly very much exaggerated.

---

[1] An excellent bibliographical article about recent works on Luther
written by John Dillenberger is available in *Church History*, June 1956,
entitled "Literature in Luther Studies, 1950-1955."

[2] H. Kerr, *A Compend of Luther's Theology*, p. xi.

If we consider the technical terminology, there is indeed a manifest difference but if we have in view the actual content and logical results of his ideas, we can scarcely reach any other conclusion than that Luther had before A.D. 1517 already grasped the conceptions and attained the points of view which gave character to his life-work."[3] The testimony of these scholars should also be kept in mind when we later consider the objection that at first Luther taught predestination but later reversed his position.

One of the important factors in the development of Luther's views was the fact that his "spiritual father" Staupitz belonged to the Augustinian monastic order. To be an Augustinian monk did not necessarily mean that one was thoroughly Augustinian in theology, but in Staupitz's case the latter was true, and as a result, the University of Wittenberg contained a definitely Augustinian emphasis. In fact, later (in 1517) Staupitz wrote a book on predestination entitled *Libellus de executione aeternae praedestinationis*, and in the same year, his book *Von der Liebe Gottes* (Of the Love of God) emphasized election and spoke of "pure, unalloyed grace." As a result of his studies in this atmosphere, Luther became acquainted with Augustine's writings under favorable circumstances. Luther himself recognized Augustine's great influence upon him; when speaking of the anonymous writing, *German Theology*, he said, "Next to the Bible and St. Augustine, no book hath ever come into my hands, whence I have learned, or would wish to learn, more of what God, and Christ, and man, and all things are." When Luther first began to grapple with the problem of predestination however, at about 1509 or 1510, he accepted the solution of the Occamists, which was common amongst the Schoolmen, that predestination is based on God's foreknowledge of man's conduct. Notes in books which Luther read at this

[3] R. Seeberg, *The History of Doctrines*, p. 223.

time, however, show that he was already leaning toward Augustine, although at first he was unwilling to accept Augustine's complete position, for example his teaching on irresistible grace. Boehmer believes that Luther's later full acceptance of Augustine's position came as a result of his reading of the *City of God*. In these early days of Luther's spiritual pilgrimage, when Staupitz was helping Luther as he struggled for inner peace, Luther was greatly agitated by the doctrine of predestination, fearing that he himself was predestined to damnation. Staupitz counseled him to avoid seeking after those things which God has hidden, but rather to look to the revelation of God's mercy which is so wonderfully displayed in Christ. In later years Luther often repeated this counsel to others who were similarly troubled.

The years which immediately preceded those in which Luther's view on predestination emerged were spent in an intensive study first of all of the Bible and secondly of Augustine. He confesses that before studying Augustine for himself he had been somewhat opposed to him, but that once he began to read the writings of that great Church Father he eagerly continued. During this period Luther's evangelical views were gradually clarified, and his view of predestination formed an integral part of them.

One of the most important writings disclosing Luther's view on the subject is his commentary on Paul's Epistle to the Romans. Luther lectured to his pupils on Romans from November 3, 1515 to September 7, 1516. This (1515) was the same year in which he became acquainted with Augustine's *On the Spirit and the Letter*, in which Augustine struck at the roots of Pelagianism. This was also *two years before* the posting of his famous Ninety-Five Theses. His commentary on Romans actually consists of the notes of these lectures. These notes remained in manuscript form and therefore virtually unstudied until they were finally printed in 1908! The fact that this important work remained unknown is one factor in the failure of many scholars to recognize Luther's Calvinism. Anything written about Luther before 1908 simply cannot do justice to Luther's position, for these notes especially from the eighth to the eleventh chapters of Romans clearly reveal Luther's "Calvinistic" position.

Commenting on Romans 8:28, "And we know that all things work together for good to them that love God, to them who are the called according to his purpose," Luther says; "This passage is the foundation on which rests everything that the Apostle says to the end of the chapter. . . . He here takes up the doctrine of predestination or election. This doctrine is not so incomprehensible as many think, but is rather full of sweet comfort for the elect and for all who have the Holy Spirit. But it is most bitter and hard for (*those who adhere to*)[4] the wisdom of the flesh. . . . If there would not be this divine purpose, but our salvation would rest upon our will or work, it would be based upon chance. How easily in that case could one single evil hinder or destroy it! But when the Apostle says: 'Who is he that condemneth' 'Who shall separate us from the love of Christ?' (8:33, 34, 35), he shows that the elect are not saved by chance, but by God's purpose and will. Indeed for this reason, God allows the elect to encounter so many evil things as are here named, namely, to point out that they are saved not by their merit, but by His election, His unchangeable and firm purpose (*of salvation in Christ*)."[5]

Luther then continues to pursue the subject by considering the place occupied by our own righteousness, our own good works, the freedom of the will, and chance. His conclusion

[4] Note: The words in parenthesis and italics in these comments are additions by J. Theodore Mueller in his translation of this commentary. These additions are often necessary to complete Luther's thought, since his comments were originally in the form of notes in the margins and between the lines of the Biblical text.

[5] M. Luther, *Commentary on the Epistle to the Romans,* trans. by J. Theodore Mueller, p. 112.

is that we must emphatically proclaim the denial of all of these assertions, just as Paul did. Luther considers that this teaching of Paul on predestination wipes out completely the wisdom of the flesh which he had partly destroyed by his previous arguments in the Epistle.

Continuing his comments on Romans 8:28, Luther mentions three factors which he believes should be considered in connection with the doctrine of divine predestination:

1. The proofs of God's unchangeable election which come to us from God's word and His works. Under proofs from God's word, Luther considers Paul's references to the Scriptural stories of God's election in the lives of Isaac and Ishmael and in the lives of Jacob and Esau. He also refers to Paul's quotations in Romans 9, verses 15 and 18. Luther then quotes John 13:18, "I speak not of you all; I know whom I have chosen," John 10:27-29, "My sheep hear my voice, and I know them, and they follow me: and I give unto them eternal life; and they shall never perish, neither shall any man pluck them out of my hand. My father, which gave them me, is greater than all; and no man is able to pluck them out of my Father's hand," and II Timothy 2:19, "The foundation of God standeth sure, having this seal, the Lord knoweth them that are his," as further Scriptural proof of this doctrine.

Then Luther continues by listing some of the works of God which he considers further proof of God's election. He mentions those that Paul mentions in this section of his epistle, that is, God's dealings with Ishmael, Esau, and Pharoah. He also describes the way in which God permits many of His people to be attacked by great enemies, and yet saves them. Finally, Luther points out that God permits some people to fall into great sin, yet He saves them. Examples of this phenomenon are David and the thief on the cross. On the other hand, others, such as Saul and Judas, begin to do good works and yet are lost.

2. The second factor which Luther considers is that all objections to predestination proceed from the wisdom of the flesh, that is, from human reason. Luther then lists and refutes the four main objections to this viewpoint:

a. In the first place, it has been alleged that man has been given a free will by which he can earn either merit or demerit. Luther replies that man's free will in itself has not the least ability to secure righteousness for the will itself is totally corrupted by sin.

b. The second objection is that predestination is inconsistent with such statements of Scripture as "Who will have all men to be saved" (I Timothy 2:4). Luther's reply is that all such statements are realized properly in the elect.

c. The third objection is that if men sin of necessity then they are unjustly condemned. To this Luther answers: We are sinners of necessity and so are under condemnation, but no one is a sinner by coercion or against his will.

d. The fourth objection which Luther considers at this point is that God's hardening of the will of man makes God the cause of man's sin and condemnation. Luther considers this to be the most powerful objection. He answers with Paul's answer that what God wills cannot be unjust, for what right has the clay to criticize the potter. Luther then makes the statement that the purpose of God's law is that the elect might obey it and the reprobates be caught in it, thus displaying both God's wrath and His mercy. To those who would object at this point by saying, "God seeks His glory at the expense of my misery," Luther answers that it is the voice of the flesh that says, "My, my," and that we must omit this emphasis on self and concern ourselves with God's glory instead.

3. The third factor which Luther here considers in connection with God's election is that it is the wisdom of the flesh to which this doctrine is so bitter, and which revolts

against it and thus becomes guilty of blasphemy. Luther states very clearly at this point that his conviction is that our salvation rests in no wise upon ourselves and our conduct, but is founded solely upon what is outside ourselves, that is, on God's election. While objections issue from human reason, this doctrine makes those who possess the wisdom of the Spirit rather than that of the flesh very happy. If the warnings in God's Word make us tremble, this is in Luther's opinion a good sign. If anyone has fears concerning whether or not he is elected and is in general troubled about his election, he should be thankful that he has such fears. So says Luther, and emphasizes the point by quoting Psalm 51:17, "The sacrifices of God are a broken spirit; a broken and a contrite heart, O God, thou wilt not despise." He then gives the practical advice that when one reaches this point he should cast himself on the faithfulness of God who makes this promise that He will despise no one with this attitude, and then no longer trouble himself about his predestination. He points out that it is not a characteristic of the reprobate but of the elect to tremble concerning the secret counsels of God.

All of the above is a summary of Luther's comment on this one verse, Romans 8:28. This shows how thoroughly Luther considered the subject and how definitely he taught the doctrine of predestination.

Some of Luther's comments on verses in the ninth chapter provide a further revelation of his thinking on the doctrine of predestination. Concerning the eleventh verse: "For the children being not yet born . . . that the purpose of God according to the election might stand, not of works, but of him that calleth," he states that the purpose of this verse is to magnify divine grace and to utterly destroy the arrogant boasting of human merit. Luther then points out that the apostle doesn't say "Neither being good or evil," but rather, "Neither having done any good or evil," for, says Luther, both sons were evil through the corruption of original sin, both were equal as far as merit is concerned, equally members of the same corrupt human race! Commenting on the fifteenth verse, "I will have mercy on whom I will have mercy," Luther states that while this is a hard saying to the proud and the prudent, it is sweet to the humble and to those who despair of themselves.

In chapter 11, in commenting on the twenty-ninth verse, "The gifts and calling of God are without repentance," Luther declares this to be an excellent statement proving that God's counsel is not changed by man's merit or demerit. Because God does not change his mind, the elect will surely be converted and come to the point where they will possess true faith.

Luther's commentary on the Epistle to the Romans gives ample proof of how enthusiastically Luther endorsed Paul's doctrine of predestination; in fact, it shows that he revelled in the doctrine because it magnified the grace of God and humbled the pride of the natural man.

In Luther's preaching in this same year (1515) a similar emphasis is in evidence. In his sermon on the Feast of St. Stephen, and in several other sermons, he speaks of the inward voice of man (*synterseis*) which urges him toward what is good. He warns, however, that belief in the existence of this voice might lead us to trust in our own strength which would be spiritually dangerous. In other sermons, he speaks of regeneration taking place without seeking, praying, or knocking on the part of man, but simply as a result of the mercy of God, and of the fact that the new birth resembles natural generation in which the child does nothing.[6]

Shortly after the conclusion of his lectures on Romans, Luther took part in the Wittenberg Disputation in 1516 on the subject: *Man's powers and will without grace.* Luther said, "Man's will without grace is not free, but captive, though

6 M. Luther, *Werke*, Weimar ed. 1, p. 10ff.

not unwillingly." In defending this position, he made several references to Scripture, for example to the passage where Jesus teaches that whosoever sins is the slave of sin, and that he only is free who is set free by the Son of God.

In fragments of his writings which are dated in the late autumn of 1516, Luther said, "I do not deny that the will is free, or rather *seems to itself* to be free by the freedom of contrariety and of contradiction with regard to its lower objects. . . . The will when confronted with temptation cannot without grace avoid falling, by its own powers it is able to will only what is evil."

On September 4, 1517, Luther took part in the *Disputation against the Theology of the Schoolmen*. Luther's position at this disputation exists in written form. Until very recently, however, it was only in Latin and German but has now been translated into English. Here is another example of how Luther's position has been partially obscured by his writing not being available to all scholars. Luther states his position in ninety-five propositions including the following:

5. It is false to state that man's inclination is free to choose between either of two opposites. Indeed, the inclination is not free, but captive. This is said in opposition to common opinion.

6. It is false to state that the will can by nature conform to correct precept. This is said in opposition to Scotus and Gabriel.

7. As a matter of fact, without the grace of God the will produces an act that is perverse and evil.

10. One must concede that the will is not free to strive toward whatever is declared good.

29. The best and infallible preparation for grace and the

sole means of obtaining grace is the eternal election and predestination of God.

30. On the part of man, however, nothing precedes grace except ill will and even rebellion against grace.

Shortly after the posting of his famous Ninety-Five Theses, Luther, commenting on Hebrews 11:6 said, "But this faith does not come from nature but from grace."[7] In another comment on Hebrews, he said, "To desire Christ and to ask for him, to look and to knock is the gift of prevenient grace, and not the choice of our will."[8]

In April of 1518, the *Disputation of Heidelberg* took place. It was arranged by friends who hoped thus to lessen the storm which had been aroused by the posting of the famous theses. In preparation for this meeting, Luther set down 28 theological theses and 12 philosophical theses. In introducing these theses, Luther says, "they have been deduced well or poorly from St. Paul, the especially chosen vessel and instrument of Christ, and also from St. Augustine, his most trustworthy interpreter." The thirteenth theological thesis states that free will since the fall exists in name only and that as long as it does what it is able, it commits mortal sin. The fourteenth thesis claims that free will since the fall is able to do good only in a passive capacity while it is always able to do evil in an active capacity. Martin Bucer, whose importance in the influence of Luther upon Calvin will be noted later, was present at this disputation.

In 1519, Luther received a copy of Huss's treatise *De Ecclesia*, which has been referred to already. When he was driven to defend Huss in the *Disputation at Leipzig*, he maintained that Huss was unjustly condemned by the Council of Constance for holding doctrines taught by Paul and by Augustine. These doctrines included Huss's definition of the

[7] M. Luther, *W.A.*, 57. 232. 26.
[8] *Op Cit.*, 57. 116. 1.

universal church as the *universitas praedestinatorum,* that is, the total number of the elect.

In August of 1519, Luther discussed the Leipzig Disputation in a paper entitled *Resolutions.* This paper included the statements: "Free-will is purely passive in every one of its acts," and "A good act comes wholly and entirely from God."

The Papal Bull of Excommunication in 1520 included a condemnation of Luther's thesis against free will at the Heidelberg Disputation. In the same year, Luther wrote a rebuttal entitled *An Argument in Defense of All the Articles of Dr. Martin Luther Wrongly Condemned in the Roman Bull (Assertio omnium articulorum)* in which he stated that his denial of free will was the fundamental article of his teaching. He also stated in the same volume: "No one has the power even to think anything evil or good, but everything takes place agreeably with stern necessity, as Wycliffe rightly taught, though his proposition was condemned by the Council of Constance." He sought to prove this by quoting the words of Jesus in Matthew 10 which speak of the fact that not even a sparrow falls to the ground without the Heavenly Father. Luther continued: "It is Pelagian to say that free will is able by means of earnest effort, to do anything good: it is Pelagian to think that the will can prepare itself for grace; Pelagian too is the principle handed down in the schools, that God gives His grace to the man who does what he can."

Luther speaks of the fact that Scripture is full of the doctrine of grace, but that in the three hundred years preceding him, no one had written on behalf of grace, while all had spoken against it. In his opinion, Ephesians 2:3, "Among whom also we all had our conversation in times past in the lusts of our flesh, fulfilling the desires of the flesh and of the mind; and were by nature the children of wrath, even as others," is the passage which best illustrates the biblical opposition to the concept of free will. Luther also quotes II Timothy 2:25, 26: "Instruct those that oppose the truth; peradventure God will give them repentance, that they acknowledge the truth; and return from the snares of the devil, by whom they are taken captive at his will." He then says, "Where is the free will here when the captive is of the devil, not indeed unable to do anything, but able to do only what the devil wills? Is that freedom, to be captive at the devil's will, so that there is no help unless God grants repentance and improvement?"[9] He then quotes his version of John 8:34 and 36, "Verily I say unto you, all they who are servants or possessions of sin; if the Son make you free, ye shall be free indeed." Luther further quotes pertinent statements from Augustine, for example, he mentions that Augustine in his work *Against Julian* rightly calls the term "free will" *servum arbitrium,* that is, a will in bondage.

In this same work, the *Assertio omnium articulorum,* Luther also says, "I wish that the word 'free will' had never been invented. It is not in the Scriptures, and it were better to call it 'self-will' which profiteth not. Or, if anyone wishes to retain it, he ought to apply it to the new-created man, so as to understand by it the man who is without sin. He is assuredly free, as was Adam in Paradise, and it is of him that the Scriptures speak when they touch upon freedom; but they who lie in sins are unfree and prisoners of the devil; yet because they can become free through grace, you call them men of free will, just as you might call a man rich, although he is a beggar, because he can become rich. But it is neither right nor good thus to juggle with words in matters of such great seriousness."[10]

Luther's emphasis on Scripture in this document is signi-

[9] *Works of Martin Luther,* Vol. III, "An Argument in Defense of All the Articles of Dr. Martin Luther Wrongly Condemned in the Roman Bull," p. 108f.
[10] *Ibid.,* p. 110f.

ficant. The original *Assertio* was written in Latin, and it must be admitted that in his German edition Luther had much less to say about free will. We have not been able with certainty to discover the reason for this, although this fact is in keeping with Luther's tendency to emphasize the doctrine much more in his arguments with scholars than when he dealt with people uneducated in theology.

The first edition of Luther's German translation of the New Testament appeared in September of 1522. In connection with this translation Luther wrote prefaces to the various Biblical books. In his preface to Romans, Luther dealt with the question of predestination. Speaking of Paul, he said:

"In chapters ix, x, and xi, he teaches concerning God's eternal predestination, from which it originally comes that one believes or not, is rid of sin or not rid of it. Thus our becoming righteous is taken entirely out of our hands and put in the hands of God. And that is most highly necessary. We are so weak and uncertain that, if it were in our power, surely not one man would be saved, the devil would surely overpower us all; but since God is certain, and His predestination cannot fail, and no one can withstand Him, we shall have hope against sin.

"And here we must set a boundary for those audacious and high-climbing spirits, who first bring their own thinking to this matter and begin at the top to search the abyss of divine predestination, and worry in vain about whether they are predestinate. They must have a fall; either they will despair, or else they will take long risks.

"But do you follow the order of this epistle. Worry first about Christ and the Gospel, that you may recognize your sin and His grace; then fight your sin, as the first eight chapters here have taught; then, when you have reached the eighth chapter, and are under the cross and suffering, that will teach you the right doctrine of predestination, in the ninth, tenth and eleventh chapters, and how comforting it is. For in the absence of suffering and the cross and the danger of death, one cannot deal with predestination without harm and secret wrath against God. The old Adam must die before he can endure this subject and drink the strong wine of it. Therefore beware not to drink wine while you are still a suckling. There is a limit, a time, and age for every doctrine."

From this passage it can be clearly seen not only that Luther believed in predestination; but that he considered it very important. We also have his valuable advice, no doubt partly resulting from his own experiences, as to how this doctrine must be carefully considered in its rightful place. His statement, "The old Adam must die before we can endure this subject" certainly gives at least a partial explanation of the antagonism which many have toward this doctrine.

In his translation of the New Testament, Luther rendered I Timothy 2:4 as "God wills that all be assisted" (Luther's German Bible still used today has the word *"geholfen"*), rather than God wills that all be saved as other translations have it. In a letter to Hans Von Rechenberg dated August 18, 1522, discussing this same verse, Luther says, "It was God's will that we should pray for all classes, preach the truth and be helpful to everyone both bodily and spiritually," but he insists that this verse does not mean that God calls all to salvation. He adds, "And even though many other passages should be brought forward, yet all must be understood in this sense, otherwise the Divine Providence (i.e., prevision, predestination) and election from all eternity would mean nothing at all, whereas St. Paul insists very strongly upon this."

In a sermon in February of 1523 based on II Peter, Luther says of the passage, "The Lord is not willing that any should perish, but that all should return to penance" (as it was

41

then translated), that this was "one of the verses which might well lead a man to believe this epistle was not written by St. Peter at all," at least here the author "fell short of the apostolic spirit." We do not agree with Luther on this, but it does show how strongly he held to "Calvinism"; he questions the authorship of the epistle because it *appears* to teach a doctrine contrary to a limited predestination.

Chapter Four

LUTHER'S "DE SERVO ARBITRIO"

Luther's expressions of his position soon brought a reaction
on the part of his Humanist friends as well as others. Even
Wolfgang, Capito spoke openly against him at this point,
as did the Humanist Mosellanus (Peter Shode) at Leipzig.
The most important development along this line, however,
was Erasmus's break with Luther. In his *Annotations on
the New Testament,* written some years earlier, Erasmus had
opposed the denial of the freedom of the will. Already in
1517, in his correspondence, Luther had mentioned reading
this statement by Erasmus and being greatly displeased by
it. Now increasing pressure was brought to bear upon
Erasmus from the papacy urging him to use the power of
his pen against Luther.

Erasmus would have preferred to remain neutral. He had
once admitted that he would sacrifice truth for the sake of
peace, and he had also said that he could have been an
Arian or a Pelagian if the creeds of the Church had taken
those positions. In a letter to Richard Pace in July 1521,
Erasmus had said that he would not risk his life for the sake
of truth, but preferred to endure evil laws because it was

43

safe to do so. The course of safety now lay in attacking Luther lest he endanger himself.

Therefore, under increasing pressure from the papacy, Erasmus attacked Luther and significantly chose the very doctrine under discussion. In 1524, he wrote his *De Libero Arbitrio* (*The Freedom of the Will*). Why did Erasmus choose to make his attack against Luther at this point? No answer can be given with certainty. Some scholars believe it was because Erasmus preferred to deal with a subject which was of little practical interest. Others feel that Erasmus considered this to be a point at which Luther was most vulnerable because it is a point so difficult for the natural man to accept. It is most likely, however, that Erasmus rightly saw that this was one of the most serious points of difference between himself and the Roman Catholic Church on the one hand, and Luther and his colleagues on the other hand. At least that was apparently Luther's interpretation of Erasmus's motive, for in his reply to Erasmus, Luther said, "You alone have gone to the heart of the problem instead of debating the papacy, indulgences, purgatory, and similar trifles. You alone have gone to the core and I thank you for it." Notice that Luther considered his position on free will (and therefore on predestination) as much more important than these other things which many today consider the important differences between Protestantism and Roman Catholicism. Luther also said in his reply, "Common sense and natural reason are highly offended that God by his mere will deserts, hardens, and damns, as if he delighted in sins and in such eternal torments, he who is said to be of such mercy and goodness. . . . I myself was once offended. . . . Natural reason, however much it is offended, must admit the consequences of the omniscience and omnipotence of God." He also said, "They are not my paradoxes, they are God's paradoxes."

Other reasons may also have contributed to Erasmus's

decision to attack Luther at the point of his position on free will. Lorenzo Valla, a scholar whose ideas were attractive to Erasmus, had written on the subject in 1440, and Vadian had just edited a copy of Valla's work in 1518. This recent event may well have brought the subject to Erasmus's attention. Furthermore the English Bishop Fisher had recently attacked Luther on the *Articles Condemned by the Papal Bull,* one article of which was that dealing with Luther's position on the freedom of the will. Some scholars believe that the English Bishop Tunstal, who charged that Luther made God the author of all evil, was the one who suggested the subject to Erasmus.

Luther's reply to Erasmus was entitled *De Servo Arbitrio (The Bondage of the Will).* This title was a phrase which Luther took directly from Augustine. The volume was written in 1525, after Luther had spent months restudying the subject. It is very lengthy; one of the English translation contains over four hundred pages. One valuable point which Luther makes concerning the importance of the subject is that, "It is not irreligious, curious, or superfluous, but essentially wholesome and necessary for a Christian to know, whether or not the will does anything in those things which pertain unto salvation."[1] "For our object is this: to inquire what free-will can do, in what it is passive, and how it stands with reference to the grace of God. If we know nothing of these things, we shall know nothing whatever of Christian matters. . . ." "Hence you see, this point forms another part of the whole of christianity, on which depends, and in which is at stake, the knowledge of ourselves, and the knowledge and glory of God."[2] "This therefore, is also essentially necessary and wholesome for Christians to know; that God foreknows nothing by contingency, but that he foresees, purposes, and does, all things according to his immutable, eter-

[1] M. Luther, *The Bondage of the Will,* p. 61.
[2] *Ibid.,* p. 62.

45

nal, and infallible will. By this thunderbolt, free-will is thrown prostrate and utterly dashed to pieces."[3]

In denying the freedom of the human will, however, Luther wishes it to be clearly understood that he is not thinking of an external compulsion which forces the will to choose contrary to its desires. He objects to the use of the term necessity as too harsh and tending to give the wrong impression of his position. He says, "But, *by necessity*, I do not mean *compulsion*; but . . . that a man void of the Spirit of God does not evil against his will as by violence, or as if he were taken by the neck and forced to it . . . but he does it spontaneously, and with a desirous willingness. And this willingness and desire of doing evil he cannot, by his own power leave off, restrain, or change. . . . But, again, on the other hand, when God works in us, the *will*, being changed and sweetly breathed on by the Spirit of God, desires and acts, not from *compulsion*, but *responsively*, from pure willingness, inclination, and accord."[4]

Luther then makes a comparison between the human will and a beast of burden. If God mounts man's will, it does as God wills, but if Satan mounts it, it does as Satan wills. Furthermore, as a beast cannot choose which rider he prefers, but rather the riders contend over who will ride the beast, so it is also with the human will.

Erasmus had in his *De Libero Arbitrio* stated that the whole subject ought not to be publicly discussed, since so much evil could proceed from the concept of the inability of the will if it was accepted by the populace. To this charge Luther first of all replies that it would be sufficient to answer that God has willed that these doctrines should be proclaimed openly. Furthermore Luther insists that it is important that this doctrine be recognized by all for God has promised grace only to the humble. He continues by saying,

[3] *Ibid.*, p. 64.
[4] *Ibid.*, pp. 97, 98.

"But a man cannot be thoroughly humbled until he comes to know that his salvation is utterly beyond his own powers, counsel, endeavours, will, and works, and absolutely depending on the will, counsel, pleasure, and work of another—that is, of God only. For if, as long as he has any persuasion that he can do even the least thing himself towards his own salvation, he retain a confidence in himself, and do not utterly despair in himself, so long he is not humbled before God; but he proposes to himself some place, some time, some work, whereby he may at length attain unto salvation. . . .

"These things, therefore, are openly proclaimed for the sake of the elect: that, being by these means humble and brought down to nothing, they might be saved."[5]

The main body of the *Bondage of the Will* consists of a long series of arguments in which Luther points out the fallacies in the usage of the Scriptures which Erasmus had proposed as proof of the freedom of the will in his book. Further arguments by Luther seek to show in what ways Erasmus has misinterpreted the Scriptures which Luther had previously set forth as proof that there is no free will in the sinner. Luther also gives a lengthy explanation of how God works evil in man without being the author of evil. In this section he explains the problem of the hardening of Pharoah's heart. To those who would ask why God does not change the hearts of all those who choose evil, Luther replies, "This belongs to those secrets of majesty, where 'his judgments are past finding out.' Nor is it ours to search into, but to adore these mysteries. If 'flesh and blood' here take offence and murmur, let it murmur, but it will be just where it was before, God is not, on that account, changed! And if numbers of the wicked be offended and 'go away,' yet, the elect shall remain."[6] He adds that he would give a similar answer to those who ask why God allowed Adam to fall, and to those

[5] *Ibid.*, p. 94.
[6] *Ibid.*, pp. 247, 248.

47

who ask why God allowed the whole human race to be infected by Adam's sin. Luther then defines God as a being whose will needs no reason for its action since it is superior to all rules or standards.

Luther admits that the teaching that the loving and merciful God, of his mere will, abandons men, hardens them, and damns them as though He delighted in their eternal torments causes great offense to common sense or natural reason, and has thus offended many great men down through the centuries. Luther confesses that he himself had often been thus offended even to such an extent that he had wished that he had never been born. Then he continues by saying that now he realizes how healthy that desperation was and how near it brought him to grace. He then discusses the case of Judas who he says both betrayed Christ willingly, and yet did what God had infallibly predetermined.

Luther definitely teaches double predestination here, for he also says, "The love and hatred of God towards men is immutable and eternal; existing, not only before there was any merit or rock of free-will, but before the worlds were made; and that all things take place in us from necessity, accordingly as he loved or loved not from all eternity."[7]

To Erasmus's assertion that the heat of controversy had driven Luther to deny free will altogether when previously he had conceded some power to the will of man, Luther replies that he is confident that an examination of his writings will prove that right from the beginning he had never made such concessions, but that he had always consistently taught that there is no such a reality as a free will.

The third and final section of Luther's writing, *The Bondage of the Will*, consists in his marshalling of further Scripture passages to strengthen his position. He prefaces this section, however, by saying, "But I shall not produce them

[7] *Ibid.*, p. 273.

all (my forces against free-will) for who could do that within the limits of this small book, when the whole Scripture, in every letter and iota, stands on my side?"[8]

In his conclusion, Luther compares the problem of free will with the problem: Why do the righteous suffer while the wicked prosper? He says that this latter problem is insoluble by the light of nature, but that it is understood in the light of grace. However, even the light of grace cannot solve the problem of how God can damn him who by his own power can do nothing but sin and become guilty. But, says Luther, the light of glory will reveal the solution. In the meantime, let the fact that the light of grace can reveal the solution to a problem that seemed unanswerable to the light of nature give us the faith to believe that an answer exists to this problem also. Let us therefore trust that although God chooses to save some of the wicked freely without merit while he damns others who are less wicked, God is a perfectly righteous God.

In 1664 Sebastian Schmidt published an edition of *De Servo Arbitrio* with copious notes aimed at trying to prove that this work of Luther was not as "Calvinistic" as it appeared to be, but as Cunningham comments, "The annotations, of course, are utterly unsuccessful in effecting the object to which they are directed, viz., proving that Luther did not, in this work, teach Calvinistic doctrines. No amount of straining or perversion is adequate to effect *that*."[9] Cunningham also says, "We have no hesitation in saying, that it can be established beyond all reasonable question, that Luther held the doctrines which are commonly regarded as most peculiarly Calvinistic."[10]

Of the *De Servo Arbitrio*, McGiffert says, that it was "the

[8] *Ibid.*, p. 337.
[9] W. Cunningham, *The Reformers and the Theology of the Reformation*, p. 84.
[10] *Ibid.*, p. 109.

most carefully written and in his own opinion the best of all his works."[11] Luther himself said many years later that it would be just as well if all his writings were discarded except his *Catechism* and the *De Servo Arbitrio*. Concerning the subject of the controversy, the freedom of the will, McGiffert says, "In attacking this particular position, Erasmus singled out the one point where Luther differed most widely at the same time with Romanists and Humanists."[12]

At the turn of this past century there was a heated debate on the subject of predestination and free will between the Missouri Synod Lutherans and other Lutherans. The viewpoints of some of the parties involved in this debate can be found in the pages of the *Lutheran Quarterly* of that period.[13] In one article, C. Stange, professor of the University of Greifswald, writes, "It has indeed, never been possible to deny that Luther in the above named book, (*De servo*), in harmony with all the rest of the Reformers, held to this doctrine. However, this unpleasant fact men have after all in various ways known how to conceal or tone down. They have either summarily revised the history and maintained, in evident contradiction to the fact, that Luther gave up this doctrine, in the later years of his life; or else they sought to excuse the Reformer by attributing the writing of the book, *de servo arbitrio* to his youth, in spite of the fact that the author was 42 years old; or else, lastly, they supposed that they could explain the extremes into which Luther had allowed himself to be drawn in this writing, on the basis of his polemical attitude."[14]

Erasmus, in turn, replied to Luther's *De Servo Arbitrio* with a work entitled *Hyperaspistes* in two volumes, one 300 pages long and the other 500 pages in length. Of this verbal duel

[11] A. C. McGiffert, *Martin Luther the Man and His Work,* p. 267.
[12] *Ibid.,* p. 266.
[13] In the following issues: Jan. 1904, p. 21; July 1904, p. 305-318; Apr. 1906, pp. 198-214.
[14] C. Stange, *Lutheran Quarterly,* July 1904, pp. 305, 306.

between Erasmus and Luther, Harnack remarks, "The medieval theology—even that which took the most severely strict view of the thought of predestination—is known to have always relaxed this thought precisely in the really *religious* aspect of it; for all the definitions, both of the Thomist and of the Scotists, issue in the end in a more or less refined synergism. . . . But for Luther the religious aspect continued to hold its central significance; it is God, that is to say, who works faith who plants the good tree and nourishes it. That which when viewed *from without* appears to be something subjective, and is therefore regarded by reason as an achievement of man, appears to him, from his keeping in view the real experience as he had passed through it, as the really objective thing, produced within him from without. This is perhaps what gives Luther his highest significance in theology, and on this account his work on the enslaved will ('De servo arbitrio') is in *one* respect his greatest."[15]

A lengthy series of sermons on Exodus was produced by Luther from 1524 through 1526. In one of these sermons, in discussing Pharoah's heart being hardened, he says, "God in this (impelling to evil) does well, and nothing wrong. But he who is thus impelled does wrong."[16] It must be admitted that Luther only made occasional references to the subject in his sermonizing.

In 1529 Luther prepared a statement which was to provide a doctrinal basis for a conference to be held at Schwabach. This statement is called the *Schwabach Articles*, of which the sixth article states, "This faith is not human, nor even possible for our strength, but is the work of God, and a gift which the Holy Ghost operates in us given us through Christ."[17]

[15] Harnack, *Op. Cit.*, VII, pp. 201-202.
[16] M. Luther, *Erl. Ed.*, XXXV, pp. 160-175.
[17] H. Jacobs, *Martin Luther*, p. 439.

Chapter Five

LUTHER'S "TABLE TALK"

Luther lectured on Galatians in 1519, in 1523, and again in 1531. He makes occasional references to the subject of free will in these lectures. For example, in commenting on Galatians 1:4, he condemns as filthy rags all talk about free will, religious orders, masses etc. In other works, he places the doctrine of free will in the same category with the more obvious facets of Roman Catholicism. Commenting on the 10th verse of the same chapter, he points out that he preaches doctrines which men hate, such as that of the natural depravity of all men and the condemnation of man's free will. Luther adds that preaching on such doctrines was also the reason why Paul was so strongly disliked by the Jews. Commenting on the two verses which follow, Luther says that he teaches that to believe in Christ is not a human achievement but the gift of God. He says that Staupitz had commended him for his doctrine because it gave glory to God alone and not to man. On the 15th verse, "And called me by his grace," Luther asks if God called Paul because of his holy life, his prayers, or his works, and his own answer is that God most certainly did not call Paul for any of these reasons, but rather by His grace alone.

Commenting on Galatians 2:16, Luther condemns the Pope and his theologians for being unable to believe that the unregenerate human nature is unable to do anything except that which is against God. Concerning Galatians 3:19, he compares himself to Paul who comforted himself with the thought that it was his duty to preach to the elect even though others were offended by his doctrine.[1]

A letter written by Luther to a Barbara Lisskirchen on April 30, 1531 is amongst the correspondence of Luther which has been preserved.[2] Evidently this lady was tormented by the question as to whether or not she was amongst the elect. Luther in his letter advises her to turn away from such thoughts and instead to look to Christ. He tells her that the proper way to deal with the question of predestination is to ask yourself if you believe in Christ. If you do believe in Christ, then be assured that you were called, and if called, be sure that you are predestinated to eternal salvation. Luther certainly does not here deny the fact of predestination, as some would imply, but rather he seeks to give the same practical pastoral advice which Staupitz had given to him many years before when he had been plunged into such deep distress over the same question.

Conrad Cordatus quotes Luther as having said in the fall of 1532 that we should be concerned with whether or not we have been baptized, whether or not we believe in Christ, and whether or not we receive the Lord's Supper, and not be concerned with whether or not we have been predestinated.[3] Again, there is no reason why this should be construed as an alteration of Luther's view, but rather as prac-

---

[1] A simplified translation of these lectures has been made by Theodore Graebner under the title *Luther's Commentary on Galatians*.

[2] Luther, *Letters of Spiritual Counsel*, p. 115f.

[3] *Ibid.*, p. 122.

tical advice to direct men away from morbid doubts concerning their own salvation.

In a Disputation on January 29, 1536, when his opponents referred to the belief of the old Churchmen in free will, Luther answered that what such men said is not to be accepted as gospel truth. In the same year, he made the statement that to assert that free will exists in man for the forming of a just judgment and a good intention is godless philosophy.

In a letter to Capito in 1537, Luther reaffirmed his position. In the same year, he composed the Schmalkald Articles, in which he defined his theological position. In one of these articles, speaking of his Roman Catholic opponents, he says, "They do not hold aright concerning Original Sin, because they say that the natural powers of man have remained entire and incorrupt, and that the reason can teach, and the heart do what is taught, and that God grants His grace when man acts, so far as he is able, according to his free will."[4]

According to a record made by John Mathesius, in June of 1540 Luther said that he had once been troubled about predestination, but that now he no longer sought to know the hidden will of God but looked only to the will of God as it is revealed in Jesus Christ. Caspar Heydenreich recorded the fact that Luther also spoke about the matter on February 18, 1542.[5] At that time, he discussed the attitude of those who said that if they were elected they would be saved no matter what they did, and if they were not elected they would be damned in spite of anything they did or failed to do. Luther's reply to those with such an attitude was that *although this is true*, this attitude would make the means of grace of no effect and therefore it is a dangerous viewpoint. He again emphasized the danger of seeking to

[4] *Schmalkald Articles,* Erlangen, 25:129.
[5] M. Luther, *Letters of Spiritual Counsel,* pp. 131f.

know the hidden will of God, and advised that one should look to the Word of God apart from which one is not supposed to know whether or not he is predestined. Proper use of the means of grace is the ground for the assurance of one's predestination.

Count Albert of Mansfield expressed the same dangerous viewpoint on absolute necessity, so Luther wrote to him on December 8, 1542. Luther again stated that while it is *perfectly true* that what God has determined must certainly come to pass, yet one must distinguish between the revealed and the secret will of God and not be troubled about the latter.

At about the same time, Luther delivered his lectures on Genesis. Referring to his *De Servo Arbitrio*, he did not retract the position he had taken in that writing, but emphasized a concern with the revealed will of God in order to avoid abusing the doctrine of predestination.

In a letter to an unknown person dated August 8, 1545, Luther gave similar advice. He advised looking to Christ in whom we find our election to be certain.

In an undated letter written to an anxious person, Luther said, "God rejected a number of men and elected and predestined others to everlasting life, such is the truth."[6] Yet in this same letter, there is a statement denying absolute predestination to hell. According to Kostlin, an authority on the life of Luther, this is the only such denial by Luther on record. There is, however, considerable question as to the authenticity of this statement in Luther's letter, and it is possible that the statement was a later addition by someone else, since Luther's position has been a constant source of embarrassment to many of his followers.

The hymns written by Luther included at least one which emphasized the inability of man and the grace of God:

---

[6] M. Luther, *Briefe*, ed. De Wette, p. 427.

Dear Christians, one and all rejoice,
With exultation springing,
And with united heart and voice
And holy rapture singing,
Proclaim the wonders God hath done,
How his right arm the victory won;
Right dearly it hath cost him.

Fast bound in Satan's chains I lay,
Death brooded darkly o'er me;
Sin was my torment night and day,
Therein my mother bore me,
Deeper and deeper still I fell,
Life was become a living hell,
So firmly sin possessed me.

My good works could avail me nought,
For they with sin were stained;
Free-will against God's judgment fought,
And dead to good remained.
Grief drove me to despair, and I
Had nothing left me but to die,
To hell I fast was sinking.

God saw, in his eternal grace,
My sorrow out of measure;
He thought upon his tenderness—
To save was his good pleasure.
He turned to me a Father's heart—
Not small the cost—to heal my smart
He gave his best and dearest.

A number of Luther's students boarded with him, and
some of them took notes on his informal remarks in the home.
These notes have been collected and form his *Table Talk*
of which several editions have been printed. Some of the
statements already mentioned are included in this collection.

Several other remarks in the *Table Talk* also warn of the danger of being troubled over one's own predestination rather than looking to the revealed will of God in Jesus Christ.[7] The extent to which Luther has been misunderstood at this point is exemplified by the indexing of one of these passages in W. Hazlitt's edition of the *Table Talk*. This passage is listed in the index under "Predestination condemned." But in the remark referred to, as in those already discussed above, Luther is not condemning predestination, he is simply pointing out one abuse of the doctrine against which we must safeguard ourselves. The Calvinist agrees with Luther in recognizing the danger of thus abusing the doctrine; in fact, Luther goes farther than many Calvinists would go in stressing necessity.

Actually the *Table Talk* contains many sayings that are consistent with the other writings of Luther which have already been considered and which teach man's lack of free will and God's predestination. For example, Luther said, "If a man asks, Why God permits that men be hardened, and fall into everlasting perdition? let him ask again: Why God did not spare his only Son, but gave him for us all, to die the ignominious death of the cross, a more certain sign of his love towards us poor people than of his wrath against us."[8] He continues by saying that man ought to contemplate God's great goodness, rather than speculate on the "whys and wherefores" of God's works. He also says, "Why God sometimes out of his divine counsels, wonderfully wise, unsearchable to human reason and understanding, has mercy on this man, and hardens that, it beseems us not to inquire. We should know, undoubtingly, that he does nothing without certain cause and counsel. Truly, if God were to give an account to every one of his works and actions, he were but a poor, simple God." If Luther did not believe in absolute

[7] Nos. XCVI and DCLXI in Hazlitt's edition.
[8] Hazlitt's edition, No. LXVI.

predestination, he certainly would not speak in that manner.

In fact, a whole section in the *Table Talk* is devoted to the subject of the freedom of the will, and in this section Luther takes the same position as he did in his commentary on Romans and in his writings against Erasmus. A few excerpts from this section will prove conclusively that this is true:[9]

CCLIX

"The very name, Free-will, was odious to all the Fathers. I, for my part, admit that God gave to mankind a free will, but the question is, whether this same freedom be in our power and strength, or no? We may very fitly call it a subverted, perverse, fickle, and wavering will, for it is only God that works in us, and we must suffer and be subject to his pleasure. Even as a potter out of his clay makes a pot or vessel, as he wills, so it is for our free will, to suffer and not to work. It stands not in our strength; for we are not able to do anything that is good in divine matters."

CCLXI

"Saint Augustine writes, that free-will, without God's grace and the Holy Ghost, can do nothing but sin; which sentence sorely troubles the school-divines. They say Augustine spoke *hyperbole,* and too much; for they understand that part of Scripture to be spoken only of those people who lived before the deluge, which says: 'And God saw that the wickedness of man was great in the earth, and that every imagination of the thoughts of his heart was only evil continually,' etc; whereas He speaks in a general way. . . .

"Without the Holy Ghost, man's reason, will, and understanding, are without the knowledge of God, which is nothing

---

[9] The numbering is again as found in Hazlitt's edition. Considerable variations exist in the several editions.

else than to be ungodly, to walk in darkness, and to hold that for best which is direct worst.

"I speak only of that which is good in divine things, and according to the Holy Scripture; for we must make a difference between politics and divinity; for God also allows of the government of the ungodly, and rewards their virtues, yet only so far as belongs to this temporal life. . . ."

CCLXII

"For we have altogether a confounded, corrupt, and poisoned nature, both in body and soul; throughout the whole of man is nothing that is good.

"This is my absolute opinion; he that will maintain that man's free-will is able to do or work anything in spiritual cases, be they never so small, denies Christ. This I have always maintained in my writings, especially in those against Erasmus, one of the learnedest men in the whole world, and thereby will I remain, for I know it to be the truth, though all the world should be against it; yea the decree of Divine Majesty must stand fast against the gates of hell.

"I confess that mankind has a free-will, but it is to milk kine, to build houses, etc., and no further. . . ."

CCLXIII

"Some new divines allege, that the Holy Ghost works not in those that resist him, but only in such as are willing and give consent thereto, whence it would appear that free-will is also a cause and helper of faith, and that consequently faith alone justifies not, and that the Holy Ghost does not alone work through the word, but that our will does something therein.

"But I say it is not so; the will of mankind works nothing at all in his conversion and justification; *Non est efficiens cause justificationis sed materialis tantum.* It is the matter on which the Holy Ghost works (as a potter makes a pot out of clay), equally in those that resist and are averse, as in St. Paul. But after the Holy Ghost has wrought in the wills of such resistants, then he also manages that the will be consenting there unto. . . .

"The sentences in Holy Scripture touching predestination, as, 'No man can come to me except the Father draweth him,' seem to terrify and affright us; yet they but show that we can do nothing of our own strength and will that is good before God, and put the godly also in mind to pray. When people do this, they may conclude they are predestinated. . . ."

This last section should especially be noted since in it Luther deals with irresistible grace; this being the only passage which we have discovered in which he *specifically* teaches that point of Calvinism.

These excerpts prove that the *Table Talk,* far from indicating a retraction from Luther's original position, strongly emphasizes the same teaching as that found in his *Commentary on Romans* and his *Bondage of the Will.* In fact, Johann Aurifaber, one of the editors of the *Table Talk,* said in 1566, concerning the section of *Table Talk* No. CCLXII which has been quoted above, "There you see, dear Christian, that it is a lie what some say and give out, more particularly the Synergists, viz.: that the dear Man of God (Luther) modified in any way his opinion on free-will, which they term hard because it is directly opposed to their heresy. And yet they boast of being Luther's disciples."

Both Kostlin and Kawerau have emphasized the fact that Luther never retracted his doctrine of the predestination of the damned as well as of the saved. Kostlin says that the "difference between his earlier and later years" is one only of the degree he keeps his theory more in the background.[10] Kawerau says that Luther asserted "with relentless logic

10 Kostlin, *Luther's Theologie,* 2:2, pp. 124, 82.

man's inability to turn to God, and did not shrink from the harshest predestinarian expressions, phrases indeed, which gave great trouble to Lutherans at a later date, and which they would gladly have seen expurged from his writings that Calvin's followers might not appeal to them."[11]

Speaking of Luther's doctrine of predestination, Jacobs states, "It appears in its most absolute form in his treatise, *De Servo Arbitrio,* and was never recalled; but in after years was constantly kept in the background, as, in fact, it was also previously, except when some exaggeration of human freedom provoked the most complete denial of all human agency in man's return to God."[12]

The above evidence makes it indisputably clear that Luther adhered with great insistence to what are today considered the main points of Calvinism, and that he did so before Calvin ever appeared on the scene. In fact Luther made a number of statements on the subject which were more extreme than any which Calvin ever made: some so extreme in fact that they brought about an inevitable reaction.

---

[11] G. Kawerau, *Deutsch-evangel. Blatter,* p. 528 n 1 (reprint p. 14).
[12] Jacobs, *Op. Cit.,* p. 355.

Chapter Six

THE OTHER REFORMERS

Having considered Luther's position, the next step in proving the thesis that originally the Reformation was completely "Calvinistic" is to examine the writings of the other early Reformers. The most outstanding Reformer next to Luther and Calvin was Zwingli.

1. Huldreich Zwingli[1]

Zwingli (1484-1531), the Swiss Reformer, was a contemporary of Luther (1483-1546), and reached his theological position before Calvin (1509-1564) began his ministry. In fact, Zwingli died before Calvin wrote his *Institutes* (first draft 1534 or 1535). Zwingli's works are best preserved in an eight-volume set edited by Schuler and Schulthess. A question arises concerning the influence of Luther upon Zwingli. Zwingli himself refused to be called a student of Luther. He said, "I am not ready to bear the name of

[1] An excellent bibliography of modern works on Zwingli can be found in *Church History*, June, 1950, entitled "Zwingli Study since 1918."

Luther, for I have received little from him. What I have read of his writings is generally founded in God's Word."[2] However, most students of the Reformation believe that Zwingli was influenced by Luther more than he would admit, perhaps more than he himself realized.

As to his viewpoint on predestination, Zwingli, like Luther, not only advocated the doctrine but considered it very important. Some students of his life consider it to be the *determinative principle in his theology*. This was true in spite of the fact that Zwingli was much more completely under the influence of humanism than were either Luther or Calvin. However, a group of Swiss scholars, for example Oskar Farner, believe that Zwingli's humanism has been overemphasized, and they see him primarily as a *biblical* theologian and reformer. Fisher says, "It is remarkable the Zwingli in his philosophy was a predestinarian of an extreme type, and anticipated Calvin in avowing the supralapsarian tenet, in this particular going beyond Augustine."[3]

Zwingli taught a thorough-going determinism, declaring that all evil as well as good is due to the causality of God. This even included the fall of Adam into sin. This rather extreme position led Neander to say, "It is therefore erroneous, that the harshest and most logical form of this doctrine was derived from Calvin."[4]

Zwingli's humanism becomes apparent in his view of original sin which he emphasized as sickness rather than guilt. However, he considered original sin to be the root of all individual sins and the reason why self-redemption is impossible.

Of election, Zwingli says, "It is election which saves."[5]

[2] H. Zwingli, *Works,* I, 254, Corpus Reformatorum LXXXIX (Zw. II), 145, 146.

[3] G. P. Fisher, *The Reformation,* p. 112.

[4] Neander, *Op. Cit.,* p. 668.

[5] Zwingli, *Works,* IV, pp. 122, 123.

"He who is covered by the shield of faith knows that he is elected of God by the very basis and firmness of his faith."[6] "It is evident that those who believed know that they have been elected; for those who believed have been elected. Election, therefore, precedes faith."[7]

Faith is "the fruit and present pledge of election, so that he who has faith already knows that he has been elected, which aforetime he did not know when he had not yet come to the fulness of faith, even though he was no less elect in the sight of God before faith was given him as after."[8]

Zwingli's emphasis on the primacy of election was so great that he believed that it was on the basis of election that not only the Old Testament saints but also the pious heathen such as Socrates were saved. He believed that God had elected them even though they never had a chance to trust in Christ. His concept of the Church followed that of Wycliffe; for him also the Church was the *numerus electorum*, the totality of the elect.

Zwingli, of course, believed in two-fold predestination. He said, "Election is attributed only to those who are to be saved; but those who are to be lost are not said to be elected, although the divine will has determined also concerning them, but for the repelling, rejecting, and repudiating of them, by which they may be our examples of justice."[9]

While speaking very emphatically himself, Zwingli warned others regarding the discussion of predestination, "Let this be stated with moderation and only seldom for few attain such heights of spiritual insight."[10]

The most elaborate and systematic description of his doctrine of predestination is found in his *De Providentia Dei*.

---

[6] *Ibid.*, IV, p. 122.
[7] *Ibid.*, IV, pp. 123, 127; III, p. 426.
[8] *Ibid.*, p. 575.
[9] *Ibid.*, IV, p. 115.
[10] *Ibid.*, IV, p. 113.

A detailed summary of Zwingli's view is available in See-berg's book on the history of doctrine.[11]

Zwingli claimed that his position was reached not on the basis of speculation but on the basis of Scripture. He was interested in the doctrine from a Reformer's viewpoint. He felt that it "abolished both free-will and merit," that it in one stroke cut off the head of the "Roman dragon of meritorious works." Furthermore, for Zwingli, election was the ground of assurance and was essential to Christian liberty and therefore to Christian living.

2. Jacques Le Fevre (Jacobus Faber)

LeFevre (1450-1536) was one of the earliest leaders at the beginning of the Reformation in France, although he himself never made a complete break with the Roman Catholic Church. In his preface to his commentary on the Pauline epistles he propounded the principles of the Reformation five years before Luther posted his famous theses at Wittenberg. He emphasized the authority of Scripture and the element of unmerited grace in redemption while he combated the concept of the meritorious value of good works. Calvin was deeply indebted to LeFevre for the form in which he expressed his views. One of LeFevre's pupils was Roussel, who in turn was one of Calvin's instructors. In LeFevre's Commentary on Paul's epistles, the same attitude is expressed which is later found in Calvin that all things, no matter how far beyond our comprehension, contribute to enhance the glory of God, while the interest of His creature is only of secondary importance. Thus, while LeFevre did not make clear pronouncements on the main points of "Calvinism,"

---

[11] R. Seeberg, *Textbook of the History of Doctrines*, pp. 313-315. Seeberg sees Zwingli as following the path of Luther in his *De Servo*, but allowing his determinism to affect his soteriology much more than did Luther. He also notices the affinity between Thomas Aquinas's thought and that of Zwingli. For Zwingli, his determinism had an increasing significance.

his emphasis provided part of the background from which Calvin later enunciated his principles.

3. Martin Bucer (Butzer)[12]

Bucer (1491-1551), who served mainly at Strassburg, played his best known role as a mediator in the Eucharistic controversy. He was at an early period influenced by Luther. He agreed with Luther and the other Reformers on the doctrine of predestination. His viewpoint was similar to Zwingli's, although he placed a greater emphasis on the glory of God which he felt was displayed in God's omnipotence both in His dealings with the saved and with the lost.

In his *De Regno Christi*, he said, "The kingdom of our Servitor, Jesus Christ, is an administration and procuring of the eternal salvation of the elect of God by which he . . . gathers his elect to himself." In his introduction to his exposition on the Epistle to the Romans, Bucer speaks of predestination, and talks about "this certain and immovable will of God concerning our salvation, which no creature is able to prevent." Of the wicked, he said, "God foresaw and destined even these to this lot before he created them." Bucer deals with the question of predestination in a letter written in reply to the queries of Italian protestants about the subject.[13]

Bucer used predestination for the practical purpose of establishing certainty in salvation. Pauck believes that Bucer's doctrine rose from "practical, sociological observation" that some men are religious while others are not, and that it did not preclude his belief in free will. Seeberg says, "The ideas of Luther were by Bucer, as by Melanchthon, recast in the forms derived by his practical aims."[14]

[12] A good bibliography of recent works on Bucer can be found in *Church History*, March 1956 entitled "Bucer Study Since 1918."

[13] See "A Letter of Martin Bucer" in *Journal of Theological Studies*, XLIV (1943) pp. 67-72.

[14] Seeberg, *Op. Cit.*, p. 393.

Bucer is especially important for our consideration because of his great influence on Calvin.[15]   Seeberg says, "Bucerism becomes but the stepping stone to Calvinism."[16] As was noted earlier,[17] Warfield says of Calvin's Augustinianism, that he received it "Most directly and in much detail from Martin Bucer into whose practical, ethical point of view he perfectly entered." Hyma[18] believes that the background for Calvin's doctrine begins with Gansfort and the Brethren of the Common Life, can be traced through Hinne Rode to Bucer and thus to Calvin.   He believes that Hinne Rode was more of a Calvinist in 1520 than Calvin was in 1535, and that Bucer went one step beyond Rode and "made Calvin a Calvinist." There is considerable difference of opinion as to the manner in which Bucer first influenced Calvin. Kampschulte's thesis that Calvin was a student of Bucer in Strassburg has been rejected by others, while Pauck believes that Calvin left Strassburg "a pupil or follower of Butzer." Some scholars think that Calvin first met Bucer at the Synod of Bern in 1537, but that a previous literary influence was felt by Calvin. Calvin himself said, "Principally I have wished to follow Bucer, man of holy memory." While Bucer clearly taught the doctrine of predestination, unlike Calvin he kept the doctrine of reprobation in the background, although he recognized the doctrine as has been mentioned above.

4. Heinrich Bullinger

Bullinger (1504-1575) was the successor of Zwingli and a contemporary of John Calvin. He studied in the School of

[15] That Bucerism was a preparation for Calvinism is the thesis of August Lang's *Calvin* (1909) and Anrich's *Bucer* (1914).   Otto Ritschl reaffirmed this viewpoint. J. W. van den Bosch wrote *De ontwikkeling van Bucer's praedestinatiegedachten voor het optreden van Calvijn.*

[16] Seeberg, *Op. Cit.,* p. 393.

[17] p. 6., note 2.

[18] See Hyma's *Renaissance to Reformation,* Chapt. XV, also his *The Christian Renaissance.*

67

the Brethren of the Common Life at Emmerich and later at the University of Cologne, a stronghold of opposition to Reformation teaching. His study of Lombard and Gratian led him to read Chrysostom, Ambrose, Origen and Augustine in whose writings he noted a great gulf between patristic teaching and the current doctrine of the Roman Catholic Church. He also read some of Luther's pamphlets at this time, which in turn inspired him to study the New Testament which together with the influence of Melanchthon's *Loci* led to his conversion to Protestantism in 1522. He taught, however, in a monastery at Kappel from 1523 to 1529. At this time, he began to struggle with the free will versus predestination problem. From 1523 onward, he knew Zwingli and worked in increasing cooperation with him until Zwingli's death in 1531. After that Bullinger became Zwingli's successor as pastor at Zurich. He carried on a very active correspondence with Luther, Calvin and other Reformation leaders.

In 1551, Bolsec, a doctor living at Geneva, instigated considerable opposition against the doctrine of predestination. On this occasion, Bullinger wrote a private letter to Calvin in which he stated, "Believe me, many are displeased with what you say in your *Institutes* about predestination, and draw the same conclusions from it as Bolsec has drawn from Zwingli's book on Providence." This letter resulted in a temporary alienation between Calvin and Bullinger. The *Consensus Genevensis*, setting forth Calvin's views, was not signed by the Zurich pastor.

Later, however, Bullinger clearly avowed the doctrine of predestination. The *Second Helvetic Confession* (1564), of which Bullinger was the principal author, clearly sets forth his belief in predestination. The article on predestination and election affirms, "God, from, eternity, predestinated or elected, freely and of his own mere grace, with no respect of men's character, the saints whom he would save in Christ, according to that saying of the apostle: 'God chose us in himself before the foundation of the world.' Not without a medium, though not on account of any merit of ours. In Christ, and on account of Christ, God elected us, so that they that are engrafted in Christ by faith are the elect, but those out of Christ are the reprobate."

On the subject of sin and free will, the *Confession* says, "Sin we understand to be that native corruption of man, derived or propagated to us all from our first parents, by which immersed in evil concupiscence and averse from good, but prone to all evil, full of all wickedness, unbelief, contempt and hatred of God, we are unable to do or even to think anything good of ourselves. In the unrenewed man there is no free will to do good, no power for performing good. The Lord in the gospel says, 'Whosoever committeth sin is the servant of sin.' The apostle Paul says, 'The carnal mind is enmity against God, for it is not subject to the law of God, neither indeed can be.' "

While clearly teaching predestination, Bullinger said that he would not dare to speak as Calvin did on reprobation, because no such doctrine was recognized by the Church Fathers. He was also infralapsarian, dismissing the curious questions "Whether God would have Adam fall, or whether he forced him to fall, or why he did not hinder his fall and such like,"[19] by saying that it is enough to know that God forbade Adam and Eve to eat of the fruit, and that He punished them for their disobedience. He said that he avoided speaking of the predestination of Adam's fall because it seemed irreconcilable with the justice of the punishment of sin. Bullinger agreed with Zwingli on the salvation of the pious heathen as a result of their election. Once again the facts clearly demonstrate that predestination was a doctrine held in common by the several Reformers.

[19] *Helvetic Confession,* Chapt. VIII.

5. John Knox

The conversion to Protestantism of John Knox (c. 1513-1572) is attributed to his study of Jerome and Augustine. He soon became a follower of George Wishart, an exponent of Reformed doctrine. Later he was under the direct influence of Calvin at Geneva. It is not surprising therefore that he also was an advocate of the doctrine of predestination. Knox was one of a number of British exiles at Geneva. These exiles had a considerable interest in this doctrine; and one of their number, Anthony Gilgy, had discussed it in his *Commentary on Malachi* in 1553, and also had written a treatise on it in 1556. Shortly after this, Knox received a request from England to reply to an Anabaptist who had written opposing the doctrine of predestination. In reply Knox wrote a lengthy (over 400 pages) treatise in 1560. The title of his book was *An Answer to the Cavillations of an Adversary Respecting the Doctrine of Predestination*, which was the most elaborate of any of Knox's writings.

In this treatise, Knox emphasized the importance of the doctrine by saying, "But yet I say, that the doctrine of God's eternal predestination is so necessarie to the church of God, that, without the same, can faith neither be truely taught, neither surely established; man can never be brought to true humilitie and knowledge of himself; neither yet can he be ravished in admiration of God's eternal goodnes, and so moved to praise him as appertaineth. . . . Then onely is our salvation in assurance, when we fynd the cause of the same in the bosome and counsell of God."[20]

Knox's method of discussing the subject was to take the statements of his adversary and answer them passage by passage. He defines prescience, providence, and predestination. He says, "Predestination, whereof how this question is, we call the eternall and immutable decree of God, by the

---

[20] D. Laing, editor, *The Works of John Knox*, pp. 24, 25.

70

which he hath once determined with himself what He will have to be done with everie man. For he hath not created all (as after shall be proved) to be of one condition."[21] He follows this by a broader definition of predestination and says, "These latter parts (to wit, of vocation, justification of faith, and of the effect of the same) have I added for such as think that we imagin it sufficient, that we be predestinate, how wickedly so ever we live. We constantly affirm the plane contrarie; to wit, that none living wickedly can have the assurance that he is predestinate to life everlasting."[22]

Knox quotes Scripture profusely throughout his treatise. The adversary against whom he was writing labelled believers in predestination "careless men," saying that they were worse than atheists. This unknown opponent had concluded his writing with these ironic words, "And as for you, Carelesse Men, you ought to take in good worth whatsoever I have said. First, because it is trueth; secondly because ye holde that all things be done of mere Necessitie, then have I written this of Necessitie."[23]

In his own concluding statement, Knox states that the result of believing in this doctrine of predestination should be that we should praise God. "To come to Christe Jesus, is neither of the runner, neither yet of the willer, but of God, who sheweth mercie to such as plesseth him: whose counselles eternal, and judgmentes most profound, can no creature apprehend and compasse; and therfore ought all the true servants of God, with reverence and with trembling saye, 'O! how incomprehensible are thy judgments, O Lord, and how unserchable are thy wayes; for of thee, by thee, and for thee, are all things. To thee be glorie for ever and ever. So be it.' "[24]

[21] Ibid., p. 37.
[22] Ibid., p. 37.
[23] Ibid., p. 465.
[24] Ibid., p. 468.

Once again it is evident that our major thesis has been justified, namely, that predestination and the doctrines associated with it were held not simply by Calvin but by the three major Reformers, Luther, Zwingli, and Calvin, as well as by the less influential leaders in the Reformation. In fact, these doctrines were maintained by Luther, Zwingli and several others before Calvin ever appeared on the scene. The predestinarian position was presented by both Luther and Zwingli in more extreme forms than it was later expressed by Calvin. These doctrines were a part of the central core of the Reformation faith.

Chapter Seven

CALVIN

Calvin's general position is so well-known that it will not be necessary to document it as in the case of the other Reformers. However, it will be of value to notice Calvin's explanations of some of the problems which arise in connection with the subject of predestination. In doing so, it is important to notice how heavily Calvin depends first of all upon the Scriptures, and secondly upon Augustine. It must also be kept in mind that Calvin was a second generation Reformer, and therefore many of the ideas which he expressed had been absorbed by him from the writings of Luther and Zwingli especially, as well as from others who had preceded him.

As Calvin's writings on the subject are studied, it becomes apparent that his was not simply an academic interest, but rather a very practical one. He was concerned with its value in producing true piety. He says, "They who shut the gates to prevent any one from presuming to approach and taste this doctrine, do no less injury to man than to God; for nothing else will be sufficient to produce in us suitable humility, or to impress us with a due sense of our great obligations to

God. Nor is there any other basis for solid confidence."[1]
All who pursue the subject do well to follow Calvin at this
point rather than to speculate as if it were merely an interesting philosophical question.

Calvin also warns of the dangers of seeking to delve too
deeply into the subject. In this, one is reminded of Luther's
emphasis. According to Calvin, the subject of predestination
is not to be considered in the spirit of idle curiosity. Men
ought to accept that which the Bible teaches on the subject,
but they ought not to speculate beyond that which has been
revealed by God. Again and again he repeats this same
principle in various ways. He says, for example, "I only
desire this general admission, that we should neither scrutin-
ize those things which the Lord has left concealed, nor
neglect those which he has openly exhibited, lest we be
condemned for excessive curiosity on the one hand, or for
ingratitude on the other."[2]

With regard to the relationship between foreknowledge
and predestination, Calvin says, "We maintain, that both
belong to God; but it is preposterous to represent one as
dependent on the other."[3] He reminds his readers of the
fact that it is incorrect to think of foreknowledge in a temporal relationship, for he says, "When we attribute foreknowledge to God, we mean that all things have been, and
perpetually remain, before his eyes, so that to his knowledge
nothing is future or past, but all things are present; and
present in such a manner, that he does not merely conceive
of them from ideas formed in his mind, as things remembered
by us appear present to our minds, but really beholds and
sees them as if actually placed before him."[4]

To the charge that God is unjust in predestinating some to

[1] J. Calvin, *Institutes of the Christian Religion*, Vol. II, p. 175.
[2] *Ibid.*, p. 175.
[3] *Ibid.*, p. 175.
[4] *Ibid.*, p. 175.

salvation and others to condemnation, Calvin's ultimate answer is to quote Paul, "O man, who art thou that repliest against God? Shall the thing formed say to him that formed it, Why hast thou made us thus? Hath not the potter power over the clay, of the same lump, to make one vessel unto honour and another unto dishonour?"[5] He rightly insists, however, that this is not his own answer but the answer of the Bible, so that those who reject it are not simply rejecting his argument, but are rejecting God's. The final answer to the charge of injustice is, according to Calvin, that it lies in God's will which is beyond our understanding. He insists also that men can be sure of this, that God is a just God, so that God's will and justice are only two names for the same reality.

Calvin insists that man must not blame God for the fall of the human race into sin. It is true that the fall was according to the appointment of Divine Providence, but it is equally true that it was man's own fault. God created man good, but by his own wickedness man corrupted his nature. Calvin therefore states, "wherefore let us rather contemplate the evident cause of condemnation, which is nearer to us in the corrupt nature of mankind, than search after a hidden and altogether incomprehensible one in the predestination of God."[6]

To the charge that the doctrine leads to slothfulness in morality, Calvin replies that to make this charge is to misunderstand the whole purpose of predestination, for the goal of election is a holy life. He goes on to quote a number of passages of Scripture which clearly enunciate this principle. He reminds those who oppose the doctrine that Paul who taught it was at the same time a zealous exhorter to holy living. As he says, "Let these zealots compare his vehemence with theirs; theirs will be found ice itself in comparison with

[5] Romans 9:20, 21.
[6] J. Calvin, *Op. Cit.*, p. 209.

his incredible fervour."[7]   Calvin himself certainly never allowed his firm conviction in predestination to lead him to moral slothfulness nor to prevent him from exhorting others most earnestly to live holy lives.   Nor was this for him at all an inconsistency.

Calvin insisted on the importance of preaching the doctrine of predestination. He said that it were better for a man not to be born than to be ignorant of this doctrine. According to Calvin, the devil has no more fit instruments than they who fight against the truth of predestination. He himself preached it, and in his preaching he sought to explain it in the most simple terms to the people.

Calvin said, "Behold God Who is liberal toward all.   For He makes His sun to shine on the good and on the bad. Only He sets aside a number of men to do them the privilege of adopting them to be His own children."[8]   In other words, he pointed out that predestination does not make God unjust, but rather that while there are many ways in which God is good to all men, He chooses to be especially good to some men to whom He gives the gift of eternal salvation.

From these few excerpts, it can be seen that Calvin taught the doctrine with moderation, and actually avoided some of the extreme statements which were made by several of the other Reformers.   One sometimes wonders if many of his critics ever actually read Calvin himself.   Calvin's spirit was certainly not one of rejoicing over the reprobation of some men.   Instead, he desired to be absolutely faithful to the entire Word of God, and to use all of its doctrines to lead God's people to a fuller measure of humility, assurance, and gratitude, and thus to bring the greatest possible glory to God.

---

[7] *Ibid.*, p. 213.
[8] J. Calvin, *Sermon on Ephesians 1;3-6.*

Chapter Eight

THE POST-REFORMATION REACTION

The preceding evidence has clearly established the fact that the doctrine of predestination was held in common by all of the leading Reformers and that it was the original position of both the main branches of the Church of the Reformation, the Lutheran as well as the Reformed. On the other hand, it is evident that the doctrine is held by relatively few Christians today. What happened to cause this large scale movement away from the doctrine of the Reformation? The purpose of this chapter is to seek to find the answer to that question. The answer is a very complex one, but certain aspects of it stand out above the others. One important factor was the defection of Melanchthon at this point, and the resulting movement of Lutheranism away from Luther's position. Another was the reaction within the Reformed Churches which was partly the result of the more extreme forms in which the doctrine came to be held in those churches. Arminius was the leader of this reaction. He in turn influenced John Wesley, whose opposition to the doctrine, combined with his great and lasting influence in the Church, caused the doctrine of predestination to become increasingly unpopular.

1. Philip Melanchthon (1497-1560)

At first Melanchthon followed Luther in his position on predestination and in his denial of the freedom of the human will. Some students of Melanchthon's theology claim that his deterministic predestinarianism was at first actually more extreme than that of Luther himself. This is amply borne out by statements in the first edition (1521) of Melanchthon's *Loci Communes*.[1] This edition of the *Loci* shows that Melanchthon followed Augustine to the ultimate conclusions of deterministic predestination. According to Melanchthon at that time, the will of man has no freedom. He based his belief completely on the Scriptures. He stated that all things that happen, happen necessarily according to divine predestination, there being no freedom of the human will. He undergirded this statement by quoting Romans 11:36, Ephesians 1:1, Matthew 10:29, Proverbs 16:4, Proverbs 20:24, Proverbs 16:9, Genesis 15:16, I Samuel 2:25, I Samuel 10:26, I Kings 12:15, Romans 9:1, Luke 12:7, and Ecclesiastes 8:17. This illustrates his scriptural emphasis.

In this first edition of his *Loci*, Melanchthon spoke against Thomas Aquinas's doctrine of contingency. Melanchthon said that it might seem foolish to some that he should discuss in the very beginning of his work a topic so difficult as predestination. But he went on to say that it really wouldn't make any difference whether he treated this subject as his first topic or his last, since it is a matter which falls into every department of his disputation. Melanchthon also said that freedom of the will must be discussed at the beginning, and that it is the truth of predestination which destroys the

[1] See C. L. Hill, *The Loci Communes of Philip Melanchthon* which is a recent translation of this important document.

78

false reliance on freedom of the will. He continues, however, by warning about the danger of filling the minds of young people with the fact that all that comes to pass is not by the plans and actions of mankind, but according to the will of God. He spoke of the Scriptural belief in predestination, and he blamed the impious theology of the "Sophists" for the fact that people shrink from this truth of Scripture.

In order to be considerate to those who believe that what he has to say about predestination is too harsh, Melanchthon investigated carefully the nature of the human will. In this investigation he sought to prove the error of the "Sophists." He then set forth a number of propositions with regard to the nature of the human will. He recognized that there is a sense in which the will has liberty, that is, it can choose to greet someone or not to greet him, to put on certain clothing or not to put it on, to eat certain food or not to eat it. But when it comes to affections, to the ability to love or not to love, to hate or not to hate, at this point the will is helpless. Melanchthon concluded by saying that the first type of freedom is of no consequence in spiritual matters because it is purity of the heart which God requires; therefore he compared those who have written concerning the defense of the freedom of the will with the Pharisees. It should be remembered that this was prior to the time that Erasmus wrote against Luther on the subject.

In this same edition of the *Loci*, Melanchthon wrote a lengthy discussion on "Original Sin" which he concluded with 20 theses. The fifth thesis demonstrated emphatically the position which Melanchthon held at this time. In this thesis he stated that man by his natural powers or faculties can do nothing but sin.

Melanchthon was, however, at heart a humanist. His inaugural address at Wittenberg had consisted of an outline of humanist studies. In reality, Melanchthon was a follower of both Luther and Erasmus. As has been already described, these two held opposing views on the doctrines of predestination and of free will. Ultimately Melanchthon was forced to choose between the two at this point, and more and more he moved toward the position of Erasmus. When he wrote his original *Loci* he was under the influence of Luther's anti-humanistic spirit. As a result he gave the Bible the supreme place as the source of authority, and he shared Luther's contempt for natural reason. But as time passed, his humanism reasserted itself, and he gave reason a place along side revelation as the bases for religious truth. The result was that he modified his view on predestination and free will. Here we find a striking example of the rationalistic basis for the rejection of the doctrine of predestination.

Already in 1524, Melanchthon began to show signs of leaning toward humanism; for he wrote to Erasmus on September 30th of that year concerning the reception of Erasmus's *Diatribe*, "Your moderation pleases us, though you have thrown on passages some grains of black salt. But Luther is so angry as to be able to get nothing out of it."[2]

In Melanchthon's exposition of Ephesians and Colossians written in 1527, an increased recognition of human freedom was already evident. However, he still maintained the position that no one can fear or love God except by the power of the Holy Spirit. Commenting on Colossians, he said that the will was able to perform civil righteousness but "the will cannot perform Christian or spiritual righteousness."

In the *Augsburg Confession*, in the formation of which Melanchthon played such a leading role, there seems to be a deliberate avoidance of the question of predestination. The *Confession* does states, however, that "the Human Will has a certain freedom for the administration of *justitia civilis;* but without the Holy Spirit it has not the power to bring forth spiritual righteousness."[3]

[2] *Corpus Reformatorum*, I, p. 675.
[3] Article 18.

In each succeeding edition of the *Loci* Melanchthon moved further and further away from his original position.[4] In the edition of 1535, he took his stand against absolute predestination, and he gave human free will a share in the work of conversion. He said, "There are three axes which concur in conversion; the Word, the Holy Spirit, and the Will, not indeed neutral, but resisting its own weakness." This position of Melanchthon is basically the synergism, that is, the working together of the Spirit of God and the will of man, which we have previously noted in the history of the doctrine. In the edition of 1543, Melanchthon went still further. In the additions which he made to the *Loci* in 1548, he swung still further in the direction of the power of the human will, although he still would not admit any merit on the part of man.

In 1559, Melanchthon, in a letter to the Elector of Saxony, said, "Both during Luther's lifetime and also later I fought against the stoical and Manichaen delusion which led Luther and others to write that all works whether good or evil, in all men whether good or bad, take place of necessity."[5] This statement not only reveals Melanchthon's own thinking, but also refutes those who claim that Luther changed his position toward the end of his life. Richard summarizes Melanchthon's position by saying, "Thus Melanchthon was the first among the Reformers to depart from the Augustinian *particularity*, and to bring out the doctrine of the universality of the offer of salvation."[6]

After Luther's death and extending beyond the lifetime of Melanchthon himself a controversy raged amongst the Lutherans. It is known as the Synergistic Controversy which resulted from Melanchthon's divergence from Luther at this

[4] The various editions of the *Loci* are available in Latin in the *Corpus Reformatorum*.

[5] *Corpus Reformatorum*, 9, p. 766.

[6] J. W. Richard, *Philip Melanchthon*, p. 235.

point. In this controversy, Matthias Flacius, Nicolas Amsdorf, Widang, and Hesshusius followed Luther's viewpoint in opposition to that of Melanchthon. At first, the majority of the Lutheran Church maintained the original Lutheran position, but gradually Melanchthon's viewpoint won the day. For example, the Formula of Concord (1580) was contradictory on this point. It supposedly opposed the teachings of Melanchthon and denied synergism. Yet it denied irresistible grace and affirmed the universality of the offer of the Gospel.

The position of the Formula of Concord amounted to conditional predestination which became the accepted Lutheran doctrine in the seventeenth century. It stated that predestination is the will of God that all who believe are saved. It said that foreknowledge deals with both the good and the evil, but that predestination deals only with salvation. Thus the large wing of the Protestant Church which is composed of the various bodies of Lutherans came to hold a position denying absolute predestination in spite of the fact that their great leader, Martin Luther, had been a strong advocate of such predestination.

2. *Jacob Arminius (1560-1609)*

The next important name in the history of the retreat from the predestinarian position is that of Jacob Arminius, a Dutch seminary professor.

To understand what happened, one must go back to the time of the original creeds of the Reformed wing of the church. These creeds were really quite moderate in their advocacy of predestination. However, the leaders of the second generation after the Reformation, Beza, Peter Martyr, Musculus, and Zanchi, were extreme supralapsarians. Arminius originally held to the doctrine of predestination, having studied at Geneva in 1582 and 1583, and having listened with great respect to the lectures of Beza. In 1589, Richard

Koornhert of Amsterdam attacked the doctrine of predestination. Koornhert's objection was that the doctrine of absolute decrees represented God as the author of sin, since such decrees made both sin and the damnation of the sinner necessary and inevitable. His book, called *Responsio ad Argumenta Bezae et Calvinae,* expressed this position. Koornhert was a layman, the Secretary of State of Holland. Lydius, a professor at Franeker, was asked to answer Koornhert's book. He in turn asked Arminius to make a refutation of Koornhert's position. However, when Arminius studied Koornhert's book, he himself was filled with doubt, and in fact went beyond Koornhert's position to a denial of the doctrine of predestination. As a result, he was required to appear before a Classical Court where Peter Plaucius was his chief opponent. Arminius denied that he was a Pelagian and was cleared of the charges against him. Later he was elected to become a professor at Leyden, where he was bitterly opposed by another professor, Gomarus. Constant dissension resulted, and finally Arminius resigned. He died in 1609. Simon Episcopius (1583-1644), who had studied at Leyden under Gomarus and Arminius, became the leader of those who held Arminius's position. Other leaders of the movement were James Uytenbogaert (1557-1644), John Van Older Barneveldt (1549-1619) who was the advocate general of Holland, and the famous Hugo Grotius (1583-1645). The issue of freedom of thought also became involved in this controversy.

In answer to the attack of the Arminians, the Calvinists defined their position under five points:[7] total depravity, unconditional election, limited atonement, irresistible grace,

[7] This controversy with the Arminians has resulted in drawing attention to these five points, and thus has erroneously caused many people to consider them the essentially distinctive feature of Calvinism. Actually the "five points of Calvinism" are only the application of the Calvinistic conception of the sovereignty of God in one area of truth. See B. Warfield, *Calvin and Augustine,* pp. 490-491.

and the perseverance of the saints. In opposition to these points, Uytenbogaert developed Five Articles: Article I, "God, by an eternal, unchangeable purpose in Jesus Christ his Son, before the foundation of the world, hath determined . . . to save . . . those who, through the grace of the Holy Ghost, shall believe on this his Son." Article II, "Jesus Christ the Saviour of the world, died for all men and for every man, so that he has obtained for them all, by his death on the cross, redemption and the forgiveness of sins; yet that no one actually enjoys that forgiveness of sins except the believer. . . ." Article III, "That man has not saving grace of himself, nor of the energy of his free will, inasmuch as he, in the state of apostasy and sin, can, of and by himself, neither think, will, nor do anything that is truly good, such as saving faith eminently is; but that it is needful that he be born again of God in Christ through his Holy Spirit." Article IV, "This grace of God is the beginning, continuance, and accomplishment of all good, even to this extent, that the regenerate man himself, without prevenient or assisting, awakening, following, and co-operative grace, can neither think, will, nor do good. . . . But as respects the mode of the operation of this grace, it is not irresistible. . . . That those who are incorporated into Christ by a true faith, and have thereby become partakers of his life-giving Spirit, have thereby full power to strive against Satan . . . if only they are ready for the conflict, and desire his help and are not inactive. . . . But whether they are capable, through negligence, of forsaking again the first beginnings of their life in Christ, or again returning to this present evil world . . . that must be more particularly determined out of the Holy Scriptures, before we ourselves can teach it with the full persuasion of our minds."

At first glance, these articles seem fairly moderate, so that many today, who would call themselves Calvinists, would find these articles quite acceptable. They are moderate when compared to later Arminianism which developed from them. However, a more careful study of these articles reveals that at the crucial points they stand opposed to true Calvinism. The first article actually bases predestination on foreseen faith, so that the choice of man and not the choice of God is the deciding factor. The second article teaches a universal grace so that again the basic decision is made by man. Again in the fourth article, grace not being irresistible, the choice again belongs to man, who may after supposedly becoming a Christian later repudiate his faith.

The Synod of Dort of 1618 and 1619 rejected these articles, and formulated the five Canons of Dort. These Canons also are moderate in their statements, and not only clearly state the Reformed position but carefully guard against the abuses of the doctrines described. For example, the Canons state: "The elect . . . attain the assurance of . . . election, not by inquisitively prying into the secret and deep things of God; but by observing in themselves . . . the infallible fruits of election . . . such as a true faith in Christ, filial fear, a godly sorrow for sin, etc." With regard to reprobation it says, "God . . . hath decreed to leave in the common misery into which they have wilfully plunged themselves . . . permitting them in his just judgment to follow their own way, which by no means makes God the author of sin." Grace is irresistible, but "does not treat men as senseless stocks and blocks, nor takes away their will and its properties, neither does violence thereto; but spiritually quickens, heals, corrects, and at the same time sweetly and powerfully bends it." The Canons clearly emphasized that this work of God "requires the use of means."

The Synod of Dort not only ratified these Canons but also deposed (over two hundred) clergymen who advocated the Five Articles. In spite of persecution, a group of Remonstrants continued their activities, and demonstrated the real root of their objections to the Reformed position by moving increasingly in the direction of rationalism. While this group never became influential, yet gradually their basic ideas permeated into many churches which theoretically maintained the historic Calvinistic position.

Two further developments in the history of the doctrine of predestination within the Reformed wing of the church ought to be considered. One was Amyraldism. Moise Amyraut (1596-1664) studied at Saumur under Cameron who opposed Arminianism but himself departed somewhat from historic Calvinism. Under this influence, Amyraut developed a position commonly called "hypothetical universalism." He first published his ideas in his *Traite de las predestination* in 1634. His viewpoint was as follows: God wills that all men be saved on condition that they believe. However, no one can fulfill this condition because of depravity. Therefore God wills that a certain number of persons be saved and that the others be passed over, which actually comes to pass as a result of God's decree. Amyraut thus places together two irreconcilable ideas. Either one or the other must be accepted, which leaves the other purely theoretical. One of Amyraut's students, Claude Pajon, was involved in further controversy on the subject, and while he claimed to be faithful to Calvinism actually robbed it of its meaning by his deistic interpretation of the mode of the operation of divine grace. Pajon's students in turn went beyond their teacher, and became either Arminian or Roman Catholic. The Swiss theologians issued the Helvetic Consensus in 1675 in oppostion to Amyraldism.

In the face of the growing Arminianism within the churches which theoretically were Calvinistic, the outstanding defense of the doctrine of predestination was made by Jonathan Edwards (1703-1758). His most important work on the subject was his *Freedom of the Will.*[8] In this volume,

[8] A new edition including a lengthy introduction by Paul Ramsey has recently been published by Yale University Press.

for which he spent years of preparation, Edwards begins by carefully defining the terms involved, including "will," "necessity," "freedom" etc. Then, at great length, and by entering into many fine philosophical distinctions, he shows the inconsistencies in the Arminian position. He then explains how acts may be "necessary" and yet either virtuous or blameworthy. In his conclusion, Edwards shows how what he has proved with regard to the freedom of the will also proves the truth of each of the other of the Five Points of Calvinism. In spite of the work of Jonathan Edwards, however, the general trend toward Arminianism continued.

3. John Wesley (1703-1791)

To understand the position of John Wesley, one must know something of the history of Calvinism in England. At the time of the English Reformation, the advocates of that Reformation were definitely Calvinistic. "The Anglican Church agreed with the Protestant Churches on the continent on the subject of predestination. On this subject, for a long period, the Protestants generally were united in opinion."[9] "The leaders of the English Reformation, from the time when the death of Henry VIII placed them firmly upon Protestant ground, profess the doctrine of absolute, as distinguished from conditional predestination."[10] The early martyrs of the English Protestant Church were predestinarians. Bradford (1510-1555), when in prison in London, disputed with certain advocates of free will. Bucer, before being called to England, dedicated his exposition of Romans, in which he set forth the doctrine of absolute predestination, to Cranmer (1489-1556). Cranmer's notes on the Great Bible show him to have been a moderate Calvinist.

Peter Martyr Vermigli (1500-1562) while teaching at Ox-

[9] Fisher, *Op. Cit.*, p. 35.
[10] *Ibid.*, pp. 35f.

ford defended the doctrine of predestination and replied to the anti-Calvinistic treatises of his predecessor Smith and to those of Pighius. The seventeenth of the *Thirty-Nine Articles* teaches the doctrine of unconditional election in the following statement: "Predestination to life is the everlasting purpose of God, whereby, before the foundations of the world were laid, He hath constantly decreed by His counsel, secret to us, to deliver from curse and damnation those whom He hath chosen in Christ out of mankind." Even Burnet, himself an Arminian, says of this article, "It is very probable that those who penned it meant that the decree is absolute."[11]

At the beginning of Elizabeth's reign, "Calvinistic teachings generally prevailed."[12] In September 1552, Bartholomew Traheron of England wrote to Bullinger regarding Calvin's writings on the subject of predestination. In this letter, he said, "We confess that he has thrown much light upon the subject, or rather so handled it as we have never before seen anything more learned or more plain."[13]

The English leaders Jewel, Nowell, Sandys and Cox all agreed with the Zurich and Genevan Reformers. In 1562, Grindal, Bishop of London, referring to Lutherans at Bremen, said, "It is astonishing that they are raising such commotions about predestination. They should at least consult their own Luther on the 'bondage of the will.' "[14] The Lambeth Articles (1595) consisted of nine statements intended to express the position of the Church on predestination in more explicit form. They were drawn up as a result of a controversy at Cambridge where Thomas Cartwright, William Perkins and William Whitaker strongly advocated Calvinism and were opposed by Peter Baro. Whitaker drew up the Lambeth Articles and they were signed by several bishops and arch-

---

[11] Burnet, *Exposition of the XXXIX Articles* (Art. xvii).
[12] Blunt, *Dictionary of Doctrinal and Historical Theology*, "Calvinism," p. 105.
[13] B. Traheron, *Original Letters*, p. 325.
[14] *Zurich Letters*, (second edition), p. 142.

bishops. The articles take a strong position on predestination, stating that "predestination to life" is not due to any good in the individual and not the result of any "foresight of faith, or of perseverance, or of good works, or of anything that is in the person predestined" but rather that the cause is "solely the good will and pleasure of God." The articles hold to a two-fold decree and imply infralapsarianism. They were rejected by the queen, but later incorporated in the Irish Articles of 1615. John Playfere, who was Baro's successor, also opposed Calvinism and wrote the first elaborate defense of the Arminian position in English.

During the reign of James I, however, the tide began to turn. At the beginning of his reign, James I had sent commissioners to the Synod of Dort to help condemn Arminianism, although he had instructed them to counsel the Dutch to greater moderation. However, later in his reign, the insistence of the Calvinists that no temporal ruler could be head of the Church caused James to turn against them. Archbishop William Laud, (1573-1645), a vigorous High-churchman, was one of the outstanding Arminians at this time, and he promoted those clergymen who had similar views and passed injunctions forbidding the clergy to preach on subjects connected with predestination. Of Laud, Fletcher said, "He was the chief instrument which, like Moses' rod, began to part the boisterous sea of Calvinism. He received his light from Arminius, but it was corrupted by a mixture of Pelagian darkness. . . . Hence, passing beyond the Scripture meridian, he led most of the English clergy from one extreme to the other."[15]

One of the outstanding leaders of Calvinism was John Owen (1616-1683), an Independent, who opposed Laud and who wrote extensively including *Display of Arminianism* in 1643, and *Doctrine of the Saints' Perseverance Explained and*

[15] *Fletcher's Works,* Vol. II, pp. 276, 277.

Confirmed in 1654. Richard Baxter (1615-1691) weakened the forces of Calvinism by advocating a modified Calvinism which caused a split amongst the dissenters. The cause of Arminianism in England was helped by such men as Jeremy Taylor (1613-1667) who was an outspoken Arminian, and John Milton (1608-1674) who was very independent in his thought on this subject as well as on all others and whose *Apology* defended the Remonstrants. As a result of these various influences Arminianism came to permeate the Church of England. Curtiss says, "Arminianism at last, in the Church of England, became a negative term, implying a negation of Calvinism, rather than any exact system of theology whatever. Much that passed for Arminianism was in fact Pelagianism. The history of English theology will show that all who have deviated from the golden mean maintained by Arminius, between Calvinism on the one hand and Pelagianism on the other, have fallen into error as to the Trinity."[16]

Thus the theological atmosphere in the Church in England was strongly prejudiced against Calvinism when John Wesley came upon the scene. Wesley's father was of this Arminian school of thought, and his mother believed likewise In the summer of 1725, Wesley and his mother exchanged several letters on the subject of predestination. Wesley wrote, "What shall I say of predestination? How is this consistent with either the Divine justice or mercy? Is it merciful to ordain a creature to everlasting misery? Is it just to punish man for crimes which he could not but commit? That God should be the author of sin and injustice (which must, I think, be the consequences of maintaining this opinion), is a contradiction to the clearest ideas we have of the Divine nature and perfections."[17]

Susannah Wesley replied to John in a letter dated August

[16] G. Curtiss, *Arminianism in History*, p. 138.
[17] Tyerman, *Life of Wesley*, Vol. I, p. 39.

18, 1725, saying, "I have often wondered that men should be so vain as to amuse themselves with searching into the decrees of God, which no human wit can fathom, and do not rather employ their time and powers in working out their salvation. Such studies tend more to confound than to inform the understanding, and young people had better let them alone. But since I find you have some scruples concerning our article 'Of Predestination' I will tell you my thoughts of the matter. . . . The doctrine of predestination as maintained by the rigid Calvinists is very shocking, and ought to be abhorred because it directly charges the Most High God with being the author of sin. I think you reason well and justly against it."[18]

John's father, Samuel, also wrote, "We cannot be satisfied by any of those Scriptures which are brought for that purpose, that there is any such *election* of a *definite number* as either puts a force on their *nature* and *irresistibly* saves them, or absolutely excludes all the rest of mankind from salvation." The doctrine of justification held by most people within the Church of England at this time and shared by Samuel and Susannah Wesley was far from that held by the Reformers. To them faith was no longer represented as the free gift of God implanted in the human soul. Instead, faith was a human act and had its place alongside other works of human endeavor. William Law and the Moravians, both of whom had great influence upon John Wesley in the early part of his life, were also Arminian in their theology.

As a result of these early influences, Wesley's understanding of the doctrine of justification by faith was actually nearer to that of the Council of Trent than it was to what he himself called "Luther's crazy solifidianism." The truth is that "Wesley had no scientific knowledge of Luther's theology."[19]

[18] *Ibid.*, p. 40.
[19] *Annual Historical Review,* Washington, Vol. XXXI, no. 2, Jan. 1926, p. 3155.

Speaking of a Calvinist, Wesley said, "I do not believe what he terms the truths of God, the doctrine of absolute predestination. I never did believe it, nor the doctrines connected with it, no not for an hour."[20]

Wesley reveals a serious ignorance of historical fact in his writings to Fletcher on the subject of predestination. There he stated that predestination was originated by Augustine out of spite for Pelagius who, says Wesley, "probably held no other heresy than you and I do now."[21] Wesley also claimed that predestination was the basic Roman Catholic position until the Council of Trent when the Roman Catholics abandoned the position which they had always held because of their opposition to Luther and Calvin. In the light of such facts, it becomes evident that from the start, Wesley was prejudiced against Calvinism by his background, and that he never had a true appreciation of the Reformation position. He did not invent his own doctrine at this point; he simply appropriated the Arminianism which had been prevalent in the Church of England for some time.

Wesley not only disagreed with Calvinism, but he fought vigorously against it. In 1741, he published "A Dialogue between a Predestinarian and his Friend," in which he sought to prove that predestinarians teach that God causes the reprobates to sin and that he created them for the purpose of being damned. He also published "The Scripture Doctrine Concerning Predestination, Election, and Reprobation" and "Serious Considerations on Absolute Predestination." In the latter of these two writings, Wesley gave his reasons for objecting to absolute predestination. They were: 1. It makes God the author of sin, 2. It makes God delight in the death of the sinner, 3. It is highly injurious to Christ, and 4. It makes preaching a mere mockery and an illusion.

One of his strongest attacks on Calvinism came in his

[20] J. Wesley, *Works*, X, pp. 378, 379.
[21] J. Wesley, *Letters*, ed. Telford.

famous sermon entitled "Free Grace" based on Romans 8:32 and delivered at Bristol. In this sermon Wesley said that predestination meant that "the greater part of mankind God hath ordained to death; . . . them God hateth; and therefore, before they were born, decreed, they should die eternally. And this He absolutely decreed because it was His sovereign will. Accordingly, they are born for this, to be destroyed body and soul in hell." In this sermon he also gave a more detailed list of his objections to the doctrine. These were:

"1. It renders all preaching vain; for preaching is needless to them that are elected; for they, whether with it or without it, will infallibly be saved. And it is useless to them that are not elected; for they, whether with preaching or without, will infallibly be damned.

"2. It directly tends to destroy that holiness which is the end of all the ordinances of God; for it wholly takes away those first motives to follow after holiness, so frequently proposed in Scriptures, the hope of future reward and fear of punishment, the hope of heaven and fear of hell.

"3. It directly tends to destroy several particular branches of holiness for it naturally tends to inspire or increase a sharpness of temper which is quite contrary to the meekness of Christ, and leads a man to treat with contempt or coldness those whom he supposes to be outcasts from God.

"4. It tends to destroy the comfort of religion.

"5. It directly tends to destroy our zeal for good works; for what avails it to relieve the wants of those who are just dropping into eternal fire.

"6. It has a direct and manifest tendency to overthrow the whole Christian revelation; for it makes it unnecessary.

"7. It makes the Christian revelation contradict itself; for it is grounded on such an interpretation of some texts as flatly

93

contradicts all the other texts, and indeed the whole scope and tenour of Scripture.

"8. It is full of blasphemy; for it represents our blessed Lord as a hypocrite and dissembler, in saying one thing and meaning another—in pretending a love which He had not; it also represents the most Holy God as more false, more cruel, and more unjust than the devil; for in point of fact, it says that God has condemned millions of souls to everlasting fire for continuing in sin, which, for want of the grace He gives them not, they are unable to avoid."

One is tempted to answer each of these objections at this point, but the answers will be found in the positive assertions which have been and will be made in other parts of this volume. This excerpt from Wesley's preaching clearly shows that he had a completely contorted concept of the Reformation position. His idea of Calvinism was certainly a caricature of the doctrine which has been held by very few of even the most extreme Calvinists.

Wesley concluded this sermon by saying: "This is the blasphemy clearly contained in the horrible decree of predestination. And here I fix my foot. On this I join issue with every asserter of it. You represent God as worse than the devil. But you say you will prove it by Scripture. Hold! what will you prove by Scripture? that God is worse than the devil? It cannot be. Whatever that Scripture proves, it never can prove this; whatever its true meaning be, this cannot be its true meaning. Do you ask, 'What is its true meaning then?' If I say, 'I know not,' you have gained nothing; for there are many scriptures, the true sense whereof neither you nor I shall know till death is swallowed up in victory. But this I know, better it were to say it has no sense at all, than to say it has such a sense as this." One hesitates to criticize so great a man as Wesley; the best we can say is that his attitude toward Calvinism stands before us as a reminder that the greatest men are blind concerning

94

certain aspects of truth. Perhaps the failure of Wesley and others like him to appreciate Calvinistic doctrine is partly the fault of Calvinists who themselves have failed to grasp the doctrine or at least to express it in as clear a form as possible.

Whitefield, who had been Wesley's colleague and who himself was a strong advocate of Calvinism, begged Wesley not to repeat or publish this "Free Grace" sermon, but Wesley did anyway. The result was a break between the two. In trying to heal the break with his friend Whitefield, Wesley explained how far he was able to go in order to reach a compromise position. He said that he believed that there were three points in debate between them: 1. Unconditional election, 2. Irresistible grace, and 3. Final perseverance. With regard to the first point, Wesley said that he believed that God has unconditionally elected certain persons to do certain work, and certain nations to receive peculiar privileges. He allowed, though he could not prove, that God "has unconditionally elected some persons, thence eminently styled 'the elect' to eternal glory."[22] But Wesley could not believe that all those who were not thus elected to glory must perish everlastingly, or that there is a soul on earth that has not a chance of escaping eternal damnation.

With regard to irresistible grace, Wesley believed that the grace which produces faith and thereby salvation is irresistible at the moment when it is received, and that most believers may remember a time when God irresistibly convinced them of sin, and other times when He acted irresistibly upon their souls. But Wesley also believed that the grace of God both before and after these moments, may be, and has been resisted, and that, in general, it does not act irresistibly, but we may comply with it or not. He said that in those eminently styled "the elect," if there be such, the grace of God is so far irresistible, that they cannot but believe and

[22] Tyerman, *Op. Cit.*, Vol. I, p. 350.

be finally saved. But he could not believe that all those must be damned in whom it does not thus irresistibly work, or that there is a soul living who has not any other grace than such as was designed of God to increase his damnation.

As to final perseverance, Wesley believed that there is a state attainable in this life, from which a man cannot finally fall and that he has attained this who is able to say, "Old things have passed away, all things in me are become new," and he did not deny that all those eminently styled "the elect" will infallibly persevere to the end.

As a result of this and other attempts at reconciliation, the break between Wesley and Whitefield was temporarily healed. However, in 1770 controversy on the subject broke out again with increased bitterness, with Wesley and Fletcher on one side and Toplady, Berridge, and Rowland and Richard Hill on the other side. Toplady, author of "Rock of Ages, cleft for me," edited a magazine called *The Gospel Magazine* which was used to propagate the Calvinistic position. In 1778, Wesley began publishing *The Arminian Magazine* which was dedicated to teaching the truth that "God willeth all men to be saved."

Charles Wesley sided with his brother and even used his poetic gift to express his view. For example, he wrote:

"Increase (if that can be) the perfect hate I feel
To Satan's HORRIBLE DECREE, that genuine child of hell;
Which feigns Thee to pass by the most of Adam's race,
And leave them in their blood, to die, shut out from saving
  grace.
O Horrible Decree, Worthy of whence it came!
Forgive their hellish blasphemy, Who charge it on the Lamb!"

Obviously, bitter feelings filled the hearts of many on both sides of this controversy.

John Wesley's position was actually somewhat on the

Calvinistic side of pure Arminianism, in that he put a much stronger emphasis on original sin and total depravity than Arminius and his followers before him had done. Wesley stressed the absolute necessity of grace, but erred in believing that this grace is given to all, thus giving everyone the power to choose between two alternatives. In other words, man's loss of free will through the fall was only hypothetical because of the effect of the atonement of Christ on all men. Although in general Wesley's attitude toward Calvinism was one of intense antagonism, there were times when he wavered. In 1771, he admitted that during the period between 1738 and 1746 he had leaned toward Calvinism. In fact, at the Methodist's Second Conference in 1745, in a series of questions and answers, this one was included: "Q. 23. Wherein may we come to the very edge of Calvinism? A. (1) In ascribing all good to free grace, (2) In denying all natural free will, and all power antecedent to grace, and (3) in excluding all merit from man even for what he has or does by the grace of God."

However, Wesley's general attitude is well described in one of his letters written to Lady Maxwell on September 30, 1788. He said, "Is not Calvinism the very antidote of Methodism, the most deadly and successful enemy which it ever had?"[23] On the other hand, Wesley did admit that there had been a degree of bigotry in his position.[24] The net result of Wesley's influence was that by his leadership of the whole Methodist movement and all of the groups influenced by Methodism, he did more than anyone else to popularize the anti-Calvinistic position.

The theological influence of Melanchthon, Arminius, and Wesley, coupled with the naturalistic spirit of modern man by which he regards himself as "the master of his fate," provide an explanation for the fact that the united stand

---

[23] J. Wesley, *Letters,* Vol. 8, p. 95.
[24] *Ibid.,* Vol. 4, p. 295.

which the Reformers had taken regarding the doctrine of predestination and the doctrines associated with it steadily lost ground. As a result, today most of Protestantism takes a synergistic position which is actually similar to that which the Roman Catholic Church held in opposition to the Reformers.

Chapter Nine

BARTH AND BRUNNER

The major departures from the Reformation doctrine of predestination, that by Melanchthon, that by Arminius, and the variation of Arminianism popularized by Wesley, have now been considered. No new departure of importance occurred until that of our present day, when neo-orthodoxy has produced a departure from the historic Reformed doctrine in an entirely new direction. This position is exemplified in the theology of the leading exponents of neo-orthodoxy, Karl Barth and Emil Brunner.

Karl Barth

Barth mentions the doctrine of election many times in his writings. He, of course, deals with it in the appropriate section of his *Romerbrief (The Epistle to the Romans)* written in 1919; although, at that time, his position was not yet fully developed. Later he discussed it in *Gottes Ghadenwahl* (1936) and in *Gotteserkenntnis und Gottesdienst nach reformatorischer Lehre (The Knowledge of God and the Service of God according to the Teaching of the Reformation)* published in 1938. However, his fully described position on election is to be found in his *Kirchliche Dogmatik (Church Dogmatics)* of which II/2 (published in 1942) is devoted to the subject.

For Barth, the doctrine stands at the very heart of theology. He considers election as the whole gospel, for it emphasizes most emphatically the key word—grace. However, he makes an entirely new approach to the doctrine compared to the traditional view which has been commonly held.[1] His position may be summed up briefly as follows: Jesus Christ is the electing God and Jesus Christ is the elect man. In election, we are not dealing with a hidden God but instead with God revealed in Christ. Barth places great emphasis on the phrase in Ephesians 1:4, "chosen *in him.*" Because of this man must never think that any element of arbitrariness exists in election, for in Christ God has revealed only a desire to save. Barth feels that theologians have not appreciated this sufficiently, that while in pastoral practice ministers have urged people to look to Christ as the source of the assurance of their election, they have not founded their actions on a solid doctrine which gives them grounds for such pastoral practice. Although Barth rejects the basic Remonstrant position, he appreciates the fact that they spoke of Christ as the foundation of election. His emphasis at this point is consistent with the extreme Christocentricity of his entire theology and with what he has said about God's perfections in the preceding volume of the *Dogmatik*.

Although Barth's position is completely new, in fact he believes the traditional doctrine needs to be completely revised, he yet finds points of agreement with other theologi-

[1] For a more complete description of Barth's position as found in his *Dogmatik*, see Otto Weber's *Karl Barth's Church Dogmatics*, pp. 93-103. For Brunner's important criticism of Barth see his *The Christian Doctrine of God*, pp. 346-352. The analysis of a more traditionally Reformed theologian can be found in Berkouwer's *The Triumph of Grace in the Theology of Karl Barth*, pp. 89-122.

ans of past ages, (which appear to be very superficial in most cases). For example, he sees the Canons of Dort agreeing with him in making election by grace the whole gospel, and he feels that Calvin sought to give a similar Christological explanation of predestination, although he failed in the attempt. He would prefer the *decretum absolutum* of Reformed theology (which he, however, rejects) to the position of Lutheranism (which is completely different from that of Luther, as we have already demonstrated). In fact, Barth is most strongly opposed to all forms of synergism, and goes beyond historic Calvinism in emphasizing the powerlessness of man. On the other hand, he finds in the Lutheran doctrine a desire to place election on a Christological basis, which he approves.

Barth's criticism of the *decretum absolutum* is that it leaves an "empty spot" where the name "Jesus Christ" ought to appear, for there is no will of God different from the will of Jesus Christ. As Barth has said: Jesus Christ is the electing God. Barth finds Scriptural ground for this position in John 1:1, 2, "In the beginning was the Word, and the Word was with God, and the Word was God. The same was in the beginning with God"; in John 13:18, "I speak not of you all: I know whom I have chosen: but that the scripture may be fulfilled, He that eateth bread with me hath lifted up his heel against me"; and in John 15:16, 19, "Ye have not chosen me, but I have chosen you, and ordained you, that ye should go and bring forth fruit, and that your fruit should remain; that whatsoever ye shall ask of the Father in my name, he may give it you. . . . If ye were of the world, the world would love his own; but because ye are not of the world, but I have chosen you out of the world, therefore the world hateth you." Barth's most serious objection to Calvin's position is that basically he made a separation at this point between God and Jesus Christ. Barth is correct in stating that there is no difference between the will of God and that of Christ; but he is wrong in assuming that the will of Christ is to save everyone. Actually, the very Scripture which he quotes to buttress his position at this point refers to the choosing out of certain individuals from the midst of a world which hates Christ and his disciples.

Concerning the controversy between supralapsarianism and infralapsarianism, Barth denies the presuppositions upon which both positions are founded, but believes the "supra" position to be closer to the truth than infralapsarianism. Already in his *Romerbrief*, he spoke appreciatively of the "supra" position. His basic reason for preferring this position is that it makes less of a separation between creation and redemption, which Barth feels ought to be considered together, for both are the work of Christ. He is concerned, however, that the "supra" position is open to the charge that it makes God the author of sin. In reality, however, in speaking approvingly of supralapsarianism he does not mean the doctrine as it has been conceived historically; for he does not believe that before the creation, God chose certain individuals out of the human race for salvation.

As to double predestination, Barth recognized both election and reprobation, but again not at all in the traditional sense. Jesus Christ is both the elect and the reprobate. In rejecting himself, God has elected man. There is a "Yes" and a "No," but God has spoken the "Yes" to man, and the "No" to himself. Here Barth returns to his idea that evil is unreal, for it is a power which has been utterly defeated.

The second section of Barth's discussion in his *Dogmatik* (the first having dealt with "the election of Jesus Christ") deals with the "election of the congregation"; for he believes that Scripture is concerned first of all with the congregation and only secondarily with the individual. His section on the congregation consists mainly of an exegesis of Romans, chapters 9 through 11.

Barth considers Israel and the Church as two aspects of

the congregation, both of which have as their purpose to witness to the grace of God. Israel is a witness to the impossibility of really resisting grace, for Christ has died for her also. Even Judas shared in election by carrying out the purpose of God.

In a third section, Barth deals with "the election of the individual." The congregation's task is to tell others that they also are elected. Since God's love is universal, Barth rejects the idea of the predestination of a certain number; instead he would leave the number of the elect indeterminate. However, he would not make this "open" number equal to the number of all men. His main reason for not doing so is that this would limit God's freedom. Barth says that the church must not preach *apokatastasis* (universal restoration), but on the other hand, we must not preach any alternative either for we cannot believe that the wickedness of man is superior to grace. In 1949, in a letter to a meeting of a convention of Reformed ministers, Barth spoke similarly, stating that it is better to preach a life-giving gospel even at the risk of the error of *apokatastasis,* rather than to preach a law that kills.

Since Barth says that all men are elect in Christ, that the basic difference between believers and unbelievers is only that the unbeliever doesn't know as yet that he is elected, and that because Jesus took upon himself the rejection of man, no man is rejected, it is difficult to see how Barth can stop short of universalism. He goes beyond the Calvinistic opposition to synergism and thus places such an emphasis on the sovereignty of grace that he seems to empty human decision of any meaning whatsoever. He says that we dare not eliminate damnation, but he fails to give any reason for not doing so; in fact, this could be the only conclusion consistent with his basic premises.

Barth's concern is to eliminate what he considers the "shadows" from the doctrine of election. He wants the gospel to be only good news and to be unclouded with any reason for causing doubt which has in practice often resulted from the preaching of the traditional doctrine of election. Barth seeks to remove the question mark which has often plagued the believer, and has sometimes weakened the church's missionary zeal; but in doing so he has also removed the question mark from the fate of the unbeliever, thus reducing human faith to meaninglessness.

While Barth denies *apokatastasis,* he refuses to come to any other conclusions; and in doing so he jeopardizes his whole position, for in claiming to solve one problem, he has replaced it with an equally serious insoluble problem. Perhaps Barth will yet clarify his position, but until he does, we must hold suspect a theology which ends in universalism, despite the unwillingness of its founder to accept its logical conclusions.

Emil Brunner

In his *Dogmatics,*[2] Brunner explains his position with regard to election and predestination in very clear terms. He considers election a very dangerous subject, yet one which lies at the very heart of our faith since it relates us to eternity. However, while he speaks highly of election, he strongly condemns all talk of predestination, and considers the latter a most serious menace to the important doctrines of the love of God and the seriousness of human decision. In Brunner's opinion, the Reformers were mistaken in distinguishing between the decrees of creation and election. The Bible doesn't speak of a decree of election; rather both creation and election are connected by the fact that the Son is the mediator of both. The similarity at this point with Barth's thought is apparent.

[2] See Brunner, *Dogmatics, Vol. I, The Christian Doctrine of God,* Section, "The Will of God," Chapter 22 "The Eternal Divine Decrees and the Doctrine of Election."

Brunner believes that the correct starting point for a proper understanding of this doctrine is to recognize that faith is a response to a personal encounter. Election for Israel meant that the nation knew its dependence upon the grace of God, so through Jesus Christ the individual Christian is also brought to a similar position. For Brunner, the elect are the ones who are called; in this, he seems to forget that many are called but few are chosen.

In further enunciating his own position, Brunner criticizes three errors which he believes he has discovered in the thinking of others. The first error is that of Barth (whom he doesn't mention by name at this point in his discussion). It consists in the idea that Jesus Christ is both He who elects and He who is elected. This error leads to universalism; while the truth is that where Christ is, there is election, and where Christ is not, no election exists.

The second error which Brunner rejects is that which was held by the Reformers. In his opinion, their failure to properly understand the doctrine was the result of their making man passive and also the result of their misunderstanding of the concept of eternity. As we have pointed out in previous chapters, the Reformers sought to avoid synergism. This, believes Brunner, was good; but in so doing, they made man purely passive and thus developed the wrong idea of election. Luther, in combatting Erasmus's erroneous concept of freedom, slipped into an unbiblical determinism. Luther was correct in seeking to teach that man is of himself incapable of faith, but according to Brunner, Luther's own explanation of this truth was also erroneous. Brunner claims that Luther was later enlightened by Scripture, and, as a result, changed his position, a claim which our research into Luther's writings fails to substantiate.

According to Brunner, the Reformers also had a misconception of eternity. This misconception was due to their failure to grasp the Biblical concept of time. They understood eternal election as something which took place before time. While recognizing that there are some Biblical terms which encourage such a concept, Brunner believes that eternal election is not something which happened very, very long ago, but rather something which comes to us now out of eternity. Brunner is certainly correct in claiming that eternity must not be conceived as having only a pre-temporal relationship with time, but, on the other hand, eternity does have a pre-temporal relationship with time as well as extending above and beyond time. In other words, eternity is not only a reality now, but it was a reality before God's creative act brought time and space into being.

The third error, which Brunner considers at length, is that of double predestination. He recognizes that inescapably election involves the concept of selection, but denies that it has anything to do with numbers. According to Brunner, in the New Testament even the idea of selection falls away, and to be elect is synonymous with to believe. In his opinion, failure to recognize this led to the error of double predestination.

Brunner considers himself a Reformed theologian, and therefore he is concerned with the fact that the doctrine of double predestination has been considered typical of the Reformed position in contrast to the Roman Catholic and Lutheran positions. He believes that Luther originally held this position, but that later without openly denying it, ceased to hold it in practice, although he himself did not realize that his viewpoint had changed. We question the historical accuracy of this analysis of Luther's development.

Brunner recognizes that Zwingli as well as Calvin clearly taught the doctrine of double predestination. He believes, possibly on sound grounds, that Zwingli arrived at the doctrine because he took as his starting point speculative theology.

Brunner has a very interesting analysis of Calvin's reasons

for accepting the doctrine, which may be summarized as follows:

The central concept of Calvin was not the Divine Omnipotence, or even the Divine Glory, but rather Election in Christ. However, Calvin was led to the doctrine of double predestination along the following route:

a. Calvin's sound emphasis on grace alone led to his belief in election. This he felt implied double predestination which he was willing to accept rather than surrender the important truth of grace alone.

b. Although the idea did not occupy a central place in his theology, Calvin did believe in Divine Omnipotence, and since the end result is judgment issuing in life for some and destruction for others, he reasoned that there must have been a decree of double predestination.

c. Calvin had great respect for Augustine, and therefore he followed him in this teaching also.

d. Having accepted the doctrine, Calvin found passages which he mistakenly believed taught double predestination, and once he believed that the Bible taught it, he was thoroughly convinced of its truth.

Brunner believes that the Bible does not teach the doctrine of double predestination, although he recognizes that a few isolated passages seem to approach that position. He recognizes that the Bible teaches that alongside of the elect there are also those not elect, that is, the reprobate, who are in the majority; but he insists that the Bible is speaking about the outcome, rather than of any decree of doom. Now while we would certainly not speak in terms of a decree of doom, is not the outcome in the hands of God? Is not the outcome what He planned it to be in eternity? Is the sovereign God surprised at the outcome?

Brunner recognizes Romans 9 as the key passage dealing

with the subject of double predestination, but he insists that this is not really dealing with the subject as it is traditionally considered, because it does not deal with individuals, but with the nation of Israel. But is not the nation composed of individuals, and are not Jacob and Esau individuals? Brunner claims that the example of Esau and Jacob does not refer to a double decree, but rather that it is an illustration that God is free to act as He will: but is that not essentially to say the same thing?

Brunner insists that not only is the double decree not in Scripture, but that it leads to an idea of God and man which is contrary to that which is given in Scripture. He says that if God planned to create two kinds of human beings, those destined for life and those destined for destruction, then we cannot worship Him as a God of love. Thus he caricatures the doctrine of predestination. He says that Calvin would answer him by saying that he believes both in predestination and in God as a God of love because the Bible teaches both, but this answer does not satisfy Brunner. He insists that this makes God the author of sin, and says that Calvin's answer to this would be that we must not draw that conclusion. Again Brunner is not satisfied with Calvin's answer.

Brunner believes that the doctrine of predestination voids human responsibility, although he recognizes that Calvin's answer to that would again be that both are taught in Scripture. Furthermore, Brunner sees no purpose in preaching if this doctrine be true. He believes that the fact that Calvin did not preach double predestination, or at least did so only rarely, and that he did not include it in his catechism is proof that he only held it as an artificial theory. Brunner is convinced that Calvin and those who have followed him have made the mistake of confusing the Biblical doctrine of election with the unbiblical doctrine of predestination.

According to Brunner, the opposite error is that of a universalism based on a doctrine of the election to salvation of all men. Brunner would not deny that this is a possibility but would strongly deny it as a certainty. He believes that this doctrine, which as we have mentioned previously is called the doctrine of *apokatastasis*, has certain features in common with that of double predestination; namely, that both deny human responsibility and both eliminate the tension between God's holiness and His love.

For Brunner, election is only rightly understood by those who hold the dialectic position of neo-orthodoxy. He holds that the doctrine of election is not intelligible in theory but only in the decision of faith; it cannot be understood in terms of doctrine but only as personal encounter. Here we discover an apparent inconsistency; Brunner insists that belief in the predestination of the saved logically leads to double predestination which logically leads to God as the author of sin, but then he is equally insistent that election which he distinguishes from predestination must not be subjected to the same laws of logic. He denies that the Bible teaches the paradox that God chooses to save some men and yet all men are responsible; but he gives the explanation of his own doctrine in terms of a paradox.

The history of the doctrine of predestination as outlined by Brunner may be summarized briefly as follows: Before Augustine there was no Christian doctrine of predestination, since the Christians were engaged in repudiating the pagan emphasis on fate, and thus emphasized human freedom and responsibility. Augustine, however, rediscovered Paul's gospel of "grace alone," but made the mistake of connecting election with the problem of human freedom (one wonders how it is possible to avoid considering the relationship between the two). Augustine, furthermore, failed to connect faith in Christ with election, but defined election as the predestination to salvation of a certain number from amongst the total lost human race. He was infralapsarian, in that he spoke of the predestination to salvation but only of the foreknowledge of reprobation. It remained for Gottschalk to place election and reprobation on an equal plane. Aquinas revived the position of Augustine, while Duns Scotus advocated Pelagianism against which Bradwardine and Wycliffe reacted. Luther and Calvin both looked at the problem as a choice between Augustinianism and Pelagianism, and thus both were led to the doctrine of double predestination.

Brunner also discusses the very point which is a major consideration in this book, that is, Luther's position. Brunner insists, contrary to our thesis, that although Luther taught strict determinism in *De Servo Arbitrio,* he later entirely changed his position, a change clearly demonstrated by Th. von Harnack in his *Luthers Theologie.* Brunner takes 1525 as the date of this turning point. Now while we agree that there was a shift in Luther's emphasis, we emphatically deny that Luther's thinking was radically changed.[3] His concern over misunderstanding the doctrine and his warnings concerning the danger of meditating on one's election or reprobation apart from God's will as it is revealed in Jesus Christ is in perfect keeping with the concerns which the strongest Calvinists also share; therefore these expressions on the part of Luther certainly cannot be considered as proof of a reversal of his earlier position.

In Brunner's estimation, Luther recognized the source of the traditional doctrine of predestination as speculative theology, while Calvin failed to realize this. Brunner sees no further development in the doctrine except that Beza, going beyond Calvin, placed the doctrine at the beginning of his dogmatics in connection with creation. The controversies between Lutherans and Calvinists, and those amongst Calvinists added nothing to a better understanding of the sub-

---

[3] See pp. 51-55 of this volume giving specific references to many statements by Luther dated long after 1525 in which he maintained his continued belief in predestination, and especially his statement that of all his writings he considered only *De Servo Arbitrio* and his catechism as worth saving.

ject. The Synod of Dort described election in infralapsarian terms. Schliermacher and Alexander Schweitzer championed Augustinianism with pantheistic modifications. Only the school of Kuyper in the Netherlands and some American Calvinists still maintain double predestination and then usually in the modified form of the articles of Dort. Thus Brunner summarizes the history of the doctrine.

Barth's position, in the opinion of Brunner, is worthy of study because his is the most detailed and comprehensive discussion of the subject in modern times and because he presents some entirely new ideas on the subject. Brunner agrees with the "main tendency" of Barth's position; that is, in basing election entirely on the Bible and rejecting the speculative thought introduced by Augustine and carried to its logical conclusion in Calvin's double decree. Barth's contribution lies in his belief that Christ is the only electing God and the only elect man. Brunner rejects this position because it makes the God-man eternally pre-existent and thus destroys the meaningfulness of the incarnation. He finds it very strange that Barth considers himself a defender of Calvin against Lutheranism and of supralapsarianism against infralapsarianism. While Barth denies being a universalist, he actually goes much farther, in Brunner's opinion, in that he teaches that Jesus is the only elect and the only reprobate, thus completely saving both believers and unbelievers from ever coming under the wrath of God. Brunner, therefore, considers Barth at this point as standing alone in opposition to the whole theological tradition, and more seriously, in opposition to the teaching of the New Testament, for he thus rejects a final judgment.

Barth's position is thus a most serious perversion of the gospel. The fault lies in Barth's basic "objectivism," that is, his desire to detract from the subjective element, faith. Barth concludes, from the fact that in Christ salvation is offered to all, that all are saved, although some do not know it yet. Thus since everything has been already decided in Christ's election, there is no real decision remaining for man to make. Brunner thus cannot see how Barth can really believe this, and therefore he hopes that Barth will yet clarify his position. Brunner's criticism of Barth is very effective, but what does Brunner himself conclude?

That question is answered in connection with Brunner's discussion of the doctrine of *apokatastasis*. Having traced the doctrine from Origen through the Reformation period Anabaptists, Denk and Hut, to Schleiermacher who held it as an hypothesis, Brunner himself rejects the doctrine, but at the same time he cannot conceive of some being eternally lost. He, however, refuses to consider these two alternatives as the only possible ones, but at the same time he fails to propose any other alternative. On the one hand, he believes that we have no right to maintain that we can be saved apart from our faith, and on the other hand, he says that we have no right to think that others will be lost although they have no faith. He claims that we must resist logical conclusions since they will lead to one of two errors, the double decree or universal salvation.

Dialectic theology seems to be very convenient, you can use logic to demolish your opponent's position, but you refuse to allow him to use logic to disprove yours! Brunner thus rejects the traditional doctrine of predestination, but he refuses to give a satisfactory alternative. He rightly warns against undue speculation, but he goes to the opposite extreme of refusing to accept the obvious implication of the Biblical doctrine which is that God has chosen some to salvation. He fails to answer, in fact he strongly insists that it is wrong to consider, the question, "Why are some saved, and others lost?" He insists on emphasizing the word "election," but doesn't mean by that word what has always been meant by it, that God has chosen certain individuals to salvation; but rather he equates it with the general concept that God has chosen to save. To Brunner, election means that the gospel is rooted in eternity, but such a use of the word adds nothing to that which we already know, for where else would it be rooted, if it is the gospel provided and proclaimed by an eternal God? Thus while Brunner strongly criticizes Barth's position, both he and Barth make of election a doctrine entirely different from that which was held by the Reformers.

Chapter Ten

THE BIBLICAL BASIS

We must now ask ourselves the question, Why is it that all of the Reformers originally maintained what are now considered to be the peculiarly Calvinistic doctrines? The answer is clear: The Reformers believed in the Bible as the Word of God, they were convinced that they found this doctrine in the Bible, and therefore they accepted it. They did not believe in picking and choosing from the Bible those parts which they approved, but were convinced that their consciences must be captive to the Word of God.

It is hardly necessary to try to prove that all of the Reformers had such an attitude toward the Scriptures. One of the great principles of the Reformation was the absolute authority of the Scriptures. For example, Luther began his *Table Talk* by saying: "That the Bible is God's Work and book I prove thus. . . ."[1] We have already seen that it was primarily Luther's study of the Bible which led him to his position. His commentaries on the Word of God contain many of his affirmations of the "Calvinistic" position. One

[1] M. Luther, *Table Talk*, p. 1.

114

of his objections to the use of the term "free will" was that it is not found in the Bible. In his *De Servo Arbitrio,* Luther strongly emphasized the doctrine of the infallibility of Scripture, and he was angered at Erasmus's assertion that the Bible contains contradictions.

The relationship between Zwingli's attitude toward Scripture and his adherence to the doctrine of predestination was similar to that of Luther. As has already been mentioned, Zwingli claimed that he reached his position not on the basis of speculation but on the basis of the teachings of the Bible. It was in their commentaries on Paul's epistles, significantly, that LeFevre and Bucer advocated the doctrine.

Calvin was simply following the other Reformers in advocating the doctrine of predestination because he found it taught in the Word of God. Even his critics will admit that Calvin taught the doctrine because he was convinced that it was the teaching of Scripture.

With this in mind, let us examine the Scriptures. Many who have done so have as a result been convinced that predestination is definitely taught in the Bible. For example, speaking of the doctrine, Warfield says, "It is not too much to say that it is fundamental to the whole religious consciousness of the Biblical writers and is so involved in all their religious conceptions that to eradicate it would transform the entire Scriptural representation."[2] James Lindsay says, "To begin with it must be said that there seems to be no evading the doctrine of an election by grace, as found both in the letter and the spirit of Scripture."[3] Snaith says, "We may not like this word 'choose' or its companion 'election.' They may be abhorrent to us, but they are firmly embedded in both Old and New Testament. Either we must accept this

[2] B. B. Warfield, "Predestination" in Hastings' *A Dictionary of the Bible,* Vol. IV, p. 48.
[3] J. Lindsay, "Predestination" in *The International Standard Bible Encyclopedia,* Vol. IV, p. 2435.

idea of choice on the part of God with its necessary accompaniment of exclusiveness, or we have to hold to a doctrine of the Love of God other than that which is Biblical."[4]

The Old Testament everywhere assumes that all things which occur are the carrying out of the plan of God. Joseph, for example, sees the evil of his brothers as a part of God's plan which has good as its ultimate goal. The Bible clearly says that God hardened the heart of Pharoah, while at the same time it states that Pharoah hardened his own heart. To say that this is simply a Hebrew form of expression is no solution to the problem, for the question then becomes, What is the fundamental idea being expressed?

Not only is this representation constantly presented in the historical section of the Old Testament, but the prophets have the same viewpoint. For example, Isaiah says, "The Lord of hosts hath sworn, saying, Surely as I have thought, so shall it come to pass; and as I have purposed, so shall it stand."[5] Jeremiah 23:20 states: "The anger of the Lord shall not return, until he have executed, and till he have performed the thoughts of his heart: in the latter days ye shall consider it perfectly." These are just a few illustrations of a thought which recurs throughout the writings of the prophets. The whole concept of predictive prophecy depends on the concept of the previous planning of God. Such larger plans are of necessity composed of many small details.

The poetic section of the Old Testament likewise contains this concept. For example, in Proverbs 8:22, 23, it is stated: "The Lord possessed me in the beginning of his way, before his works of old, I was set up from everlasting, from the beginning or ever the earth was."

According to the Old Testament, God has a plan for the whole world. Included in this larger plan, He had a special plan for the nation of Israel. The people of Israel were His

4 N. Snaith, *The Distinctive Ideas of the Old Testament*, p. 139.
5 Isaiah 14:24.

peculiar possession as a result of His choosing, and this choosing was not because of any goodness in them, or of any other attractive qualities which they had, but on the contrary: "The Lord did not set his love upon you, nor choose you, because ye were more in number than any people; for ye were the fewest of all the people."[6] "Not for thy righteousness or for the uprightness of thine heart, dost thou go to possess their land: but for the wickedness of these nations the Lord thy God doth drive them out from before thee, and that he may perform the word which the Lord sware unto thy fathers, Abraham, Isaac, and Jacob. Understand therefore, that the Lord thy God giveth thee not this good land to possess it for thy righteousness; for thou art a stiffnecked people."[7] The passage in Ezekiel 16 describing God's choice of Israel when she was a bloody new born baby without any attractiveness but rather a most repulsive sight teaches this same truth. If predestination depended upon the foreknowledge of goodness, surely God would never have chosen Israel. Yet if there is one fact clearly presented in the Old Testament it is this: Of all the nations of the world, God chose Israel to be the recipient of great spiritual blessings. "Blessed is the nation whose God is the Lord: and the people whom he hath chosen for his own inheritance."[8]

This sovereign control of God extends also to the individual. "The king's heart is in the hand of the Lord, as the rivers of water he turneth it whithersoever he will."[9] As Warfield says: "That the acts of free agents are included in this 'productive foreknowledge,' or rather in this all-inclusive plan of the life of the universe, created for the Old Testament writers apparently not the least embarrassment. This is not because they did not believe man to be free—throughout the

[6] Deuteronomy 7:7.
[7] Deuteronomy 9:5, 6.
[8] Psalms 33:12.
[9] Psalm 33:12.

117

whole Old Testament there is never the least doubt expressed of the freedom or moral responsibility of man—but because they did believe God to be free, whether in His works of creation or of providence, and could not believe He was hampered or limited in the attainment of His ends by the creatures of His own hands. How God governs the acts of free agents in the pursuance of His plan there is little in the Old Testament to inform us; but *that He governs them in even their most intimate thoughts and feelings and impulses is its unvarying assumption.*[10] (Italics are ours).

Turning now to the New Testament, the doctrine of God's sovereign control and choice is also to be found throughout these writings as an underlying assumption. The great doctrine of providence whereby God causes all things great and small to work out for the good of His children is inescapably related to the previous choice of such individuals to be His children.

In the teachings of Jesus are to be found both the concept of the general control of God and His specific choice of His people, a choice which is not dependent on any merit of their own. Turning to the Synoptics, there are a number of passages in which Jesus speaks of His elect, His chosen ones. For example, "Except that the Lord had shortened those days, no flesh should be saved; but for the elect's sake, whom he hath chosen, he hath shortened the days,"[11] and "shall not God avenge his own elect."[12] The Parable of the Laborers in the Vineyard teaches that God is not unjust if He graciously gives to some people more than they deserve, while He deals with others in strict justice.

John's Gospel, which speaks of God's love for the world, at the same time emphasizes even more strongly than the Synoptics Jesus's teaching of God's selective choice. "The

[10] B. Warfield, *Biblical and Theological Studies*, p. 282.
[11] Mark 13:20.
[12] Luke 18:7.

118

Son quickeneth whom he will."[13] "No man can come unto me, except it were given unto him of my Father."[14] "I speak not of you all: I know whom I have chosen."[15] In the High Priestly Prayer, Jesus says, "I pray for them: I pray not for the world, but for them which thou hast given me; for they are thine."[16] Jesus also taught the doctrine of the perseverance of the saints, when He said, "And I give unto them eternal life; and they shall never perish, neither shall any man pluck them out of my hand. My Father, which gave them me, is greater than all; and no man is able to pluck them out of my Father's hand."[17] "As thou hast given him power over all flesh, that he should give eternal life to as many as thou hast given him."[18]

In the Acts of the Apostles, the same doctrine is apparent. In the days immediately after Pentecost, it is stated that the Lord added to the church those who were saved (the phrase "such as should be saved" is not an accurate translation, but indicates the definitely Calvinistic viewpoint of the translators of the King James Version). Later in Acts, conversion is described in these terms, "As many as were ordained to eternal life believed."[19] Of Lydia, it is said, "Whose heart the Lord opened, that she attended unto the things which were spoken of Paul."[20]

The clear teachings of Paul's Epistles convinced the Reformers of the doctrine. Here they found their key doctrine of justification by faith alone, and here also they found predestination. In Paul's Epistles, man's inability, God's grace, and the doctrine of predestination are woven together in one inseparable fabric. This truth is found in many Pauline

[13] John 5:21.
[14] John 6:65.
[15] John 13:18.
[16] John 17:9.
[17] John 10:28.
[18] John 17:2.
[19] Acts 13:48.
[20] Acts 16:14.

119

passages, but the three primary ones are Romans 8:29, 30, Romans 9-11, and Ephesians 1:1-12. Since Luther's comments on these passages have already been considered, it will not be necessary to study them further.

In James, it is written, "Of his own will begat he us with the word of truth,"[21] and "Hath not God chosen the poor of this world rich in faith."[22]

Peter speaks of Christians as the "elect according to the foreknowledge of God"[23] and as "a chosen generation,"[24] while of the lost he says, "them which stumble at the word, being disobedient: whereunto also they were appointed."[25]

In his Second Epistle, John wrote to "the elect lady,"[26] while in the Revelation, mention is made again and again of those whose names are written in the Book of Life from the foundation of the world and also of those whose names are not thus written.

After even such a brief survey of the Biblical material, it is difficult to understand how anyone can accept the whole Bible as the Word of God and yet reject the concept of predestination.

To approach the subject from another direction, let us briefly consider the Biblical basis for each of the "five points of Calvinism." For these points are really five facets of one consistent doctrine, and each Biblical passage supporting one point thus also supports the others. For if men are totally incapable of saving themselves (total inability or total depravity), then first of all an act of God's part is required in order to save them (unconditional election). If God only chose to save part of the human race, then it was for this portion specifically that Christ died (limited atonement).

21 James 1:18.
22 James 2:5.
23 I Peter 1:2.
24 I Peter 2:8.
25 I Peter 2:8.
26 II John 1:1.

If God chose these and Christ died for their salvation, God will not be frustrated in accomplishing their salvation (irresistible grace), and surely then they shall never be lost (perseverance of the saints). Let us then consider some of the clearest passages of Scripture supporting each of these points, at the same time seeking to interpret as fairly as possible those passages which apparently contradict these points.

1. Total inability or depravity: The strongest passages teaching this doctrine are those which speak of the spiritual deadness of the natural man. "And you hath he quickened, who were dead in trespasses and sins,"[27] and "Even when we were dead in sins, hath quickened us together with Christ (by grace ye are saved)."[28] The whole point of these passages is that the dead are absolutely powerless, therefore an act of God was necessary to bestow the gift of life. A similar analogy is drawn between birth and salvation. For example, "Except a man be born again,[29] he cannot see the kingdom of God,"[30] "Except a man be born of water and of the Spirit, he cannot enter into the kingdom of God."[31] Certainly no person has any choice between being conceived and born, or not being conceived and born. No passages of Scripture even appear to deny this truth, therefore it is not denied by those who base their doctrines on the Bible. For example, Wesley accepted this doctrine completely, he believed that but for the grace of God, everyone was hopelessly and helplessly lost, but he also believed that God grants such grace to all men and that they have the power to choose to accept it or not.

2. Unconditional election: Several passages place special emphasis on the fact that election doesn't depend on any

[27] Ephesians 2:1.
[28] Ephesians 2:5.
[29] The word here translated "again" can also be translated "from above."
[30] John 3:3.
[31] John 3:5.

differences between individuals who are chosen and those that are passed by. A most powerful one, and one which also has much practical religious value, is the one which convinced Augustine, "For who maketh thee to differ from another? and what hast thou that thou didst not receive? now if thou didst receive it, why dost thou glory, as if thou hadst not received it?"[32] Another passage is that which speaks of Jacob and Esau. ("For the children being not yet born, neither having done any good or evil, that the purpose of God according to election might stand, not of works, but of him that calleth.")[33] How could this truth be stated more clearly? Many other passages teach election, some of which we have already considered.

Other passages, however, can be found in the Scriptures which seem to contradict the fact that God has just chosen part of the human race to salvation. For example, I Timothy 2:4 says, "Who will have all men to be saved, and to come unto the knowledge of the truth." Mention has already been made of the fact that Luther deliberately translated this, "all men to be helped" thus indicating his interpretation of the difficulty. Calvin's interpretation, found in his commentary, is that from the context it can be demonstrated that God is speaking here not of individuals but of classes of men. This seems to be the best explanation. In other passages of the New Testament the word "all" is often used not of every single individual but rather in the sense of many.[34] The "all" passages prove too much; for if they are to be pressed literally then they would consistently lead beyond Arminianism to Universalism. A somewhat more difficult passage is II Peter 3:9, "The Lord is not slack concerning his promise as some men count slackness; but is

---

[32] I Corinthians 4:7.
[33] Romans 9:11.
[34] For illustrations of such usage, see H. Buis, *The Doctrine of Eternal Punishment*, pp. 114, 115.

longsuffering to us-ward, not willing that any should perish, but that all should come to repentance." We have already noted that Luther considered the sentiment of this verse so opposed to Apostolic doctrine that as a result he questioned the Petrine authorship of this epistle. Calvin comments on this verse as follows: "So wonderful is his love towards mankind, that he would have them all to be saved, and is of his own self prepared to bestow salvation on the lost. . . . But it may be asked, If God wishes none to perish, why is it that so many do perish? To this my answer is, that no mention is here made of the hidden purpose of God, according to which the reprobates are doomed to their own ruin, but only of his will as made known to us in the gospel. For God there stretches forth his hand without a difference to all, but lays hold only of those, to lead them to himself, whom he has chosen before the foundation of the world."[35] The intent of this Scripture passage is that God delays the second coming of Christ in order to give added opportunity to men to repent. God does this because He does not rejoice in the punishment of the sinner, at the same time other passages of Scripture tell us that in His justice He allows such punishment to fall upon them.

Another class of passages are those which say "whosoever will" or "whosoever believeth" will be saved. The explanation of such passages is that the natural man at enmity with God *will not*, the sinner of himself does not want to be saved (although he may desire to escape punishment). Only those who are elect, and therefore only those whose hearts have been made new by the work of God's Spirit are the "whosoever" who will desire to come to Christ for salvation.

3. Limited Atonement: In John 10:11, Jesus says, "I am the good shepherd: the good shepherd giveth his life for the

---

[35] J. Calvin, *Commentaries on the Catholic Epistles,* pp. 419, 420.

sheep." The context indicates that these sheep are true believers. Acts 20:28 speaks of "the church of God, which he hath purchased with his own blood." The angel said to Joseph, "And she shall bring forth a son, and thou shalt call his name JESUS: for he shall save his people from their sins."[36] Paul is speaking specifically to Christians when he says, "He that spared not his own Son, but delivered him up for us all."[37] In each of these passages the effects of the atonement are related to a limited group, those who are saved. Luther said, "Christ did not die absolutely for all, for he said 'This is my blood which is shed for many'—he does not say, for all, 'to the remission of sins.' "[38]

Other passages seem to connect the atonement to all men. For example: "God so loved the world that he gave his only begotten son." As one studies the usage of the term "world" in the New Testament, it becomes evident that this term is defined in several different ways. These variations of definition preclude the necessity of the term meaning every individual in each instance of its usage. The best explanation for such passages as the one cited above is that thus reference is being made to the fact that the plan of salvation now includes all nations as opposed to God's limiting his dealings almost exclusively with one nation as in the Old Testament dispensation. Commenting on the passage, "And he is the propitiation for our sins: and not for our's only, but also for the sins of the whole world,"[39] Calvin says, "Here a question may be raised, how have the sins of the whole world been expiated? . . . They . . . have said that Christ suffered sufficiently for the whole world, but efficiently for the elect. This solution has commonly prevailed in the schools. Though then I allow that what has been said is true, yet I deny that

---

[36] Matthew 1:21.
[37] Romans 8:32.
[38] M. Luther, *W.A.*, 56: 385. 29.
[39] I John 2:2.

124

it is suitable to this passage; for the design of John was no other than to make this benefit common to the whole Church. Then under the word *all* or whole, he does not include the reprobate, but designates those who should believe as well as those who were then scattered through various parts of the world."[40]

Centuries before the time of Calvin, Ambrose had given a similar explanation, when he said, "There is a certain *special universality* of the elect, and fore-known, separated and discerned from the generality of all, that a whole world might seem to be saved out of a whole world; and all men might seem to be redeemed out of all men."[41]   Calvin is correct in attributing the "sufficient for all, efficient for the elect" explanation to the Schoolmen.   Lombard wrote, "Christ offered himself to God, the Trinity for all men, as it respects the sufficiency of the price; but only for the elect as it regards the efficacy thereof, because he effected, and purchased salvation only for those who were predestinated."[42]   Thomas gave a similar explanation when he said, "The merit of Christ, as to its sufficiency, extends equally to all, but not as to its efficacy, which happens partly on account of free will, and partly on account of the election of God, through which the effects of the merits of Christ are mercifully bestowed upon some, and withheld from others according to the just judgment of God."[43]

The passage, "Who gave himself a ransom for all"[44] can be explained in the same way that I Timothy 2:4 was explained above.   Yet another explanation for all of these passages may be this: Could it not be that there are benefits, although not the benefits of eternal salvation, which accrue to the non-elect

[40] J. Calvin, *Op. Cit.,* p. 173.
[41] As quoted by Zacharias Ursinus in his *Commentary on the Heidelberg Catechism,* p. 222.
[42] Z. Ursinus, *Op. Cit.,* p. 224.
[43] Z. Ursinus, *Op. Cit.,* p. 224.
[44] I Timothy 2:6.

as a result of the death of Christ? Certainly there are many indirect benefits which have come to the lost as a result of the effects of the Christian religion which is based on the crucifixion of Christ. Not only that, but it may be that God deals more graciously with the non-elect (although He does not grant them the gift of eternal life) than He would otherwise have done, had not Christ died.

A strong argument in favor of limited atonement is this: Justice requires that punishment be meted out only once for a crime. If Christ died for all men, and yet some men were punished for their sins, then both they and Christ would have suffered for the same sins. This would be unjust, therefore Christ died only for the elect. He has suffered for the sins of believers, while the sinner who remains in unbelief suffers for his own sins.

4. Irresistible grace—First of all, it must be recognized that there are gracious workings of the Holy Spirit which may be resisted.[45] Even the believer may grieve or quench the Holy Spirit. The term "irresistible grace" refers specifically to that one gracious working of the Holy Spirit whereby He regenerates or quickens one dead in trespasses and sin. Irresistible grace follows inevitably from total inability. As has previously been mentioned, the dead cannot resist if One with sufficient power chooses to make him alive, nor can the child resist being conceived and born. The raising of Lazarus from the dead is a splendid illustration of this truth. Before Jesus spoke the word of power, Lazarus could not choose to make himself alive, and when Jesus spoke the word of power, Lazarus could not resist and choose to remain dead. So also with one who is spiritually dead, one dead in sin.

---

[45] Acts 7:51, "Ye stiffnecked and uncircumcised in heart and ears, ye do alway resist the Holy Ghost: as your fathers did, so do ye."

5. Perseverance of the Saints—The outstanding proof text[46] for this doctrine is John 10:28, 29, "And I give unto them eternal life: and they shall never perish, neither shall any man pluck them out of my hand. My Father, which gave them me, is greater than all; and no man is able to pluck them out of my Father's hand." The same truth is clearly implied in Romans 9:38, 39, "For I am persuaded, that neither death, nor life, nor angels, nor principalities, nor powers, nor things present, nor things to come, nor height nor depth, nor any other creature, shall be able to separate us from the love of God, which is in Christ Jesus our Lord."

Several passages, at a first glance, seem to imply the possibility of those who are saved yet being lost. For example, in Romans 14:15 we read, "But if thy brother be grieved with thy meat, now walkest thou not charitably. Destroy not him with thy meat, for whom Christ died." But this does not necessarily mean that the weak brother will actually be lost. The tense of the Greek verb used here is that describing a process rather than the completion of that process. Even the Lutheran commentator Lenski, who is quite ready to speak against Calvinism in discussing other passages, points out that Paul shrinks from using the aorist[47] which would describe the complete destruction of the weak brother's soul, "as if he would not say that such soul murder were possible among Christians." Moule points out that as far as the offending brother is concerned he seems to care not if he is pushing his weaker brother farther down the slope which leads to ruin. At the same time Moule states that the Lord

---

[46] Many object to using proof texts, but of course they themselves use them, for it is impossible to buttress an argument with Biblical authority without quoting specific passages of Scripture. The important thing is to quote with regard to context including the wider context of the place of the verse quoted in relation to the total Biblical revelation.

[47] If the aorist (which is a tense of the verb in Greek) had been used here, it would have described the action as having been completed.

127

may counteract such action and thus not allow the process to go on to completion.[48]

A similar passage is found in I Corinthians 8:11, "And through thy knowledge shall the weak brother perish, for whom Christ died?" Neither of these two passages is intended to speak to the question of the perseverance of the saints, but rather both are practical exhortations intended to contrast the great love of Christ for the weak brother, a love so great that He gave His life, with the lack of love of the Christian who cares so little for the salvation of his fellow Christian that he would permit the most serious spiritual consequences to fall upon his weak brother, just for the sake of satisfying the appetite of his own stomach.

Of a somewhat different nature is the following verse: "But there were false prophets also among the people, even as there shall be false teachers among you, who privily shall bring in damnable heresies, even denying the Lord that bought them, and bring upon themselves swift destruction."[49] Commenting on this verse, Lenski says, "Here we have an adequate answer to Calvin's limited atonement; the Sovereign, Christ, bought with his blood not only the elect but also those who go to perdition. Calvin does not accept this epistle as canonical; in his extensive commentary on the New Testament it is not treated. May this clause, perhaps, have been a reason for this omission?"[50] This verse does raise a difficulty; perhaps the best explanation is that these false prophets did claim to be Christians, they did consider themselves as having been bought by the Lord, and therefore their wickedness was all the more serious.

We have not considered all of the verses which bear on

[48] *The Expositor's Bible,* Vol. 5, p. 612.
[49] I Peter 2:1.
[50] Although Calvin did have doubts with regard to the authorship of II Peter, the fact is that he did write a commentary on this epistle. Lenski probably made this error because Calvin's commentary follows that on James rather than being in the same order as the books are in the Bible.

the subject, either those that prove, or apparently disprove the Calvinistic doctrines. The verses we have considered, however, are illustrative of the Biblical teaching. Although there are a few individual verses which are difficult to interpret in the light of the Calvinistic teachings, the preponderance of the Biblical evidence, both in the underlying presuppositions of all of Scripture and the teachings of individual passages, is in favor of the doctrines of absolute predestination and the other doctrines which are consistent with it. The Reformers above all sought to be true to Scripture, and in so doing they were predestinarians.

Chapter Eleven

AN EXPLANATION TO THE MODERN MIND

Having considered the position of the Reformers and the Biblical material upon which that position was based, it now remains for us to summarize what we have learned, and in so doing, try to explain the doctrines of Calvinism in terms which the modern laymen can understand.

First of all, it must be recognized that while most people err seriously by rejecting or neglecting these doctrines it is also possible to overemphasize them. The doctrine of predestination is a part—an important part—of our Biblical faith, but it can be stressed too much, as well as too little. Furthermore, it must receive a different emphasis depending on the spiritual condition of the people to whom one is speaking or writing. If we do this, we will follow the pattern laid down by the Reformers, who stressed the doctrine of predestination on the level of scholarship where the most careful distinctions must be made, but recognized that it was a difficult doctrine for those young in the faith. To do so is not to hesitate in proclaiming the whole counsel of God, but is a matter of feeding our flocks that food which is best for their particular spiritual level. Both Calvin and Luther gave this teaching a large place in their thinking, but they did not ride it as a "hobby." Only a very small fraction of the voluminous writings of Calvin deals with the subject. Luther made a valuable observation when he said that we must digest the first eight chapters of Romans before we are ready for the ninth. To overemphasize the doctrine is to warp the Biblical message just as truly as to underemphasize it. Furthermore, it is always the extreme which produces the reaction; the extremist, therefore, is apt to defeat his own purpose.

Furthermore, we must recognize that we with our finite minds must not think that we can fully comprehend the doctrine. Both Luther and Calvin warn against any such attempt. If the works of God could be comprehended by our little minds, they would be unworthy of the Almighty God whom we worship. This explanation will not satisfy the mind of the rationalist who makes the human mind the measure of all things, but it will satisfy the humble mind that bows before the majesty of God.

Another important point to realize is that God not only predestines the end but He also predestines the means to that end. He not only chooses a man for salvation. but He ordains that the preaching of the Gospel of Jesus Christ should be the means to that end.[1] He ordains that our faith and our repentance should be included in those means. This invalidates the argument that preaching is useless. Preaching is of utmost importance, because it is the God-ordained means to a God-ordained end. In fact, a right understanding of this doctrine is an encouragement to those interested in the salvation of souls. Often when preaching the Gospel, we meet hard-hearted people, and we are inclined to say, "What's the use, we shall never be able to change them," but this doctrine teaches us that there may be among these seem-

[1] L. Boettner, *The Reformed Doctrine of Predestination*, p. 254ff.

ingly most hopeless cases some whom God has ordained to salvation, and that through our preaching of His Word He can, and in some cases He will, soften the hardest hearts. The fact is that thorough-going "Calvinists" such as Paul, Luther, Calvin, Whitefield, Edwards, Tennatt, Brainerd, Bunyan, Newton, and Spurgeon have been at the same time amongst the most zealous preachers of the Gospel.

Some have the erroneous idea that predestination means that there are individuals who want to be saved but can't because they have not been predestined to salvation. This is to completely misunderstand the doctrine. The state of depravity into which all men are born is such that no one of himself desires salvation. Only after the Holy Spirit has regenerated a soul does there come the sincere desire for salvation, so that such a desire is one of the signs that an individual is amongst the elect. No one who wants to be saved is lost because of predestination.

God not only predestinates men unto salvation, but He also predestinates that the ultimate end of that salvation should be holiness of life. This undermines the argument of those who say that the doctrine leads to slothfulness of spiritual life. Those who think that they are saved because they believe that they are elect but who are not seeking a holy life are deceiving themselves, they have no Biblical reason for believing that they have been elected. For when a man is predestined to eternal life, God's Spirit works in his heart, and God's Spirit is the *Holy Spirit*. When a man is saved, God gives that man spiritual life, and spiritual life involves holiness. What God has joined together let not man put asunder! The beginning, God's choice in eternity, and the end, a holy life, are inseparable. For holiness of life is God's ultimate goal for the redeemed; His purpose is not simply to snatch souls from hell, but to present them faultless before the throne of God.

Another important point to keep in mind is that we do not

132

know who the elect are, except where we see in individuals the fruits of godliness which gives us good reason to believe that they are among the elect. A danger which has been involved in believing in the doctrine of election is that some groups have often considered that they, and they alone, are the elect. But this is not a part of the Biblical doctrine. Belonging to a certain church, or denomination, or group of denominations, is no assurance of election. Conversely, every church must recognize that the elect are to be found in other churches as well as their own, including churches whose members do not believe in the doctrine of election!

Something should be said in answer to the charge that predestination is an injustice on the part of God. The answer to this charge is that God could justly condemn all men, but in His mercy He saves some. In fact, there is such a thing as common grace; God actually treats all men with mercy, but He grants saving grace, that is, even greater mercy, to those whom He chooses to save. The doctrine of reprobation presents a real problem. We believe that the two extreme solutions to this problem which have been advanced by some groups are both incorrect. One extreme solution says that there is no such thing as reprobation. The other says that the election of some and the reprobation of others stands on an equal footing. The fact is that God chooses some unto salvation; inescapably by not choosing the remainder for salvation He is choosing to allow them to go the way in which they desire to go, which leads to their perdition. However, God delights to save; His decree to save some people is carried out with joy on His part. If we catch something of the nature of God in the face of Jesus Christ, then it is certainly with sadness that He allows the reprobates to go their own way to their destruction. We should recognize that at this point we touch the edge of the mystery involved in this doctrine, but we believe that this is the best way to understand it. Furthermore, in considering the charge of injustice, it should be recognized that the lost do not desire to be saved. It is true that they would like to escape the punishment of sin, but they love their sin and they do not desire loving fellowship with the one true God. They would not enjoy heaven, for they have no heavenly desires. God cannot be considered unjust in letting them go the way of their own desires. Furthermore, the harshness is taken from the doctrine of reprobation if we do not think of hell in terms of literal fire, but in terms of a most terrible spiritual reality which is the inescapable result of an ungodly life.[2]

We should realize that Arminianism does not really escape the charges laid against Calvinism. For both Arminians and Calvinists believe that God is omnipotent and that He is loving, and yet that some men are lost. The Arminian charges that the Calvinist teaches that God deliberately lets some go to hell. But if God is omnipotent and he foreknows that some will go to hell, as the Arminian will agree, and yet God does nothing about it, the Arminian is faced with the same problem as is the Calvinist. In fact, from this viewpoint the Calvinist's concept of God is a God of greater love, for He made certain that some should be saved, while according to the Arminian, God left it up to man, and according to this procedure it might have been that none or very few would have been saved. To leave the choice entirely in man's power, as the Arminian understands God's plan, would thus not have been a more loving way of dealing with mankind.

An inescapable connection exists between the doctrine of predestination and the most comforting doctrine in the Scriptures, that of Providence. If all things are to work together for good for the Christian, certainly then he will never cease to be a Christian, and furthermore, God must be in control of all things including the actions of all human beings. God's

---

[2] See H. Buis, *The Doctrine of Eternal Punishment.*

choice of who shall be Christians is part of His total plan, and it is the fact that God has a total plan both for the whole course of history and for each individual Christian which is our great source of comfort. Take this away and the doctrine of Providence is hopelessly crippled and one of the greatest sources of consolation for the Christian is lost.

A very definite connection also exists between the doctrine of predestination and the doctrine of prayer. The opponent of Calvinism says that the doctrine of predestination makes prayer meaningless. This is not so. As with preaching, prayer is a means. God ordains the salvation of individuals, and He also ordains preaching and prayer as two means toward their salvation. We cannot expect salvation without the use of these means which are equally a part of God's plan as salvation itself. The fact is that the Arminian would make all prayer for objects which involve the choices of men to be meaningless. Of what use is it to pray to God for someone's salvation if God has no control over it? Why talk to God about the problem if the choice belongs only to the lost soul for whom we are concerned?

Calvin's great interest in the doctrine was that it provides the strongest grounds for the assurance of salvation. Assurance is most important, and the doctrine of election necessarily carries with it that of the perseverance of the saints, which gives such assurance. It is important to realize, however, that no one has any reason to believe that he is amongst the elect unless he sees a measure of the fruits of the Spirit in his own life. Thus, predestination gives no reason for false assurance. Seeing such fruit, however, the Christian knows that although against his desire he may slip, he will not fall away completely because his continuance in the Christian faith rests not in his weak will but in the same Lord who began a good work in him.

Pride is one of the greatest sins, humility one of the greatest virtues. A right understanding of the doctrine of predestination produces humility. It is true that there have been groups who have seemed proud that they were amongst the elect. In spite of all of their emphasis on election, such groups have failed to understand the doctrine aright. Election undercuts all spiritual pride, which is the worst form of pride. Ultimately the question is this: How is it that I am a Christian and others are not? The non-Calvinist's answer is inescapably this: I was better or wiser than the people who did not become Christians, for it was my choice which made the difference. Herein lies pride. The Calvinist's answer to the same question is: There was nothing good in me, there was no reason within myself why I became a Christian and others did not; it was by the choice of God, and not my own doing. Herein lies humility.

Most important of all, we find here the root of true gratitude which in turn becomes the most powerful motive for Christian service. I am a Christian. I am experiencing every day the joy of salvation, the peace of sins forgiven, the assurance of everlasting life and all of the other wonderful facets of salvation. I look around me and see thousands of people who have not these blessings. I realize that I could just as well be like them, for it is only by God's grace that I have these wonderful reasons for joy. As a result, I am overwhelmed by God's goodness to me. I know that I owe Him everything. I know that I must seek in my whole life to please Him in order to try to express my gratitude. I know also from His Word that He desires to use me as an instrument in bringing this glorious salvation to others. Oh how good God has been to me, for my salvation, right from its very beginning, has been all a result of His grace. "Bless the Lord, O my soul, and all that is within me, bless His holy name!"

BIBLIOGRAPHY

BIBLIOGRAPHY

AMBROSE: *De fide.*
In Luc.

ANRICH, G. A.: *Bucer.* 1914.

AUGUSTINE: *De an. et ejus orig.*
De correctione et gratia.
De dono perseverantiae.
De praedestinatione sanctorum.
Exposito quarumdam propositionum ex Epistola ad Romanos.
John Ev. Tract.
Lib. i. quaestio.

BABINGTHEN, J. H.: *The Reformation.* London: John Murracy Co., 1901.

BAVINCK, H.: *The Doctrine of God.* (tr. by W. Hendriksen). Grand Rapids: Wm. B. Eerdmans Publ. Co., 1951.

BERKHOF, L.: *The History of Christian Doctrines.* Grand Rapids: Wm. B. Eerdmans Publ. Co., 1949.

BERKOUWER, G. C.: *The Triumph of Grace in the Theology of Karl Barth.* Grand Rapids: Wm. B. Eerdmans Publ. Co., 1956.

BLUNT, J.: "Calvinism" in *Dictionary of Doctrinal and Historical Theology.*

BOETTNER, L.: *The Reformed Doctrine of Predestination.* Grand Rapids: Wm. B. Eerdmans Publ. Co., 1941.

BRUNNER, E.: *Dogmatics* Vol. I. (*The Christian Doctrine of God,* tr. by Olive Wynn). London: Lutterworth Press, 1949.

BUIS, H.: *The Doctrine of Eternal Punishment.* Philadelphia: Presbyterian and Reformed Publ. Co., 1957.

Burnet, G.: *Exposition of the XXXIX Articles.* 1699.

Calvin, J.: *Commentaries on the Catholic Epistles.* Grand Rapids: Wm. B. Eerdmans Publ. Co., 1948.

   Institutes of the Christian Religion (tr. by John Allen, 2 vol.). Philadelphia: Presbyterian Board of Christian Education., 1936.

   Sermons on Ephesians.

Cunningham, W.: *The Theology of the Reformation.* Edinburgh: T. and T. Clark. 1866.

Curtiss, G.: *Arminianism in History.* Cincinnati: Cranston and Curts, 1894.

Dillenberger, J.: "Literature in Luther Studies, 1950-1955" in *Church History,* June 1956.

Edwards, J.: *Freedom of the Will* (ed. by Paul Ramsey). New Haven: Yale University Press, 1957.

Fisher, G. P.: *The Reformation.* New York: Chas. Scribner Sons, 1896.

Fletcher, J. W.: *Fletcher's Works* (Vol. II).

Harnack, K. G. A.: *History of Dogma.* (tr. by Neil Buchanan, 7 vols.) Boston: Little, Brown and Co., 1907.

Hill, C. L.: *The Loci Communes of Philip Melanchthon.* Boston: Meador Publ. Co., 1944.

Hunter, A. M.: *The Teaching of Calvin.* London: James Clarke and Co., 1950.

Hyma, A.: *The Christian Renaissance.*

   Renaissance to Reformation. Grand Rapids: Wm. B. Eerdmans Publ. Co., 1951.

Jacobs, H. E.: *Martin Luther.* New York: G. P. Putnam's Sons, 1898.

Kerr, H.: *A Compend of Luther's Theology.* Philadelphia: Westminster Press, 1943.

Kawerau, P. G.: In *Deutsch-evangel. Blatter.*

Knox, J.: *Works* (ed. by David Laing, 6 vols.). Edinburgh, 1864.

Kostlin, J.: *Luthers Theologie.* (2 vols.). Stuttgart, 1901.

Lang, A.: *Calvin.* 1909.

Lenski, R. C. H.: *The Interpretation of the Epistles of St. Peter St. John and St. Jude.* Columbus: Wartburg Press, 1945.

Lindsay, J.: "Predestination" in *The International Standard Bible Encyclopedia.* Vol. IV. Grand Rapids: Wm. B. Eerdmans Publ. Co., 1946.

Luther, M.: *The Bondage of the Will.* Baltimore: John D. Toy, 1837.

Briefe (ed. by W. M. L. DeWette and J. I. Seidemann, 6 vols.). Berlin, 1825-56.

Commentary on the Epistle to the Romans (tr. by J. Theodore Mueller). Grand Rapids: Zondervan, 1954.

Commentary on St. Paul's Epistle to the Galatians (tr. by T. Graebner). Grand Rapids: Zondervan.

Letters of Spiritual Counsel (ed. and tr. by T. G. Tapert). Philadelphia: Westminster Press, 1955.

Luther's Works (Erlangen Ed. by J. G. Plochmann and J. K. Irmischer, German treatises 67 vols., Latin treatises 38 vols.). Erlangen, 1826-1886.

Luther's Works (Weimar Ed. by J. C. F. Knaake and others) 1883 sqq.

Table Talk (ed. by Hazlitt). London: George Bell and Sons, 1902.

Works of Martin Luther (Philadelphia Ed.) Philadelphia: Board of Publication, United Lutheran Church in America, 1932.

McGIFFERT, A. C.: *Martin Luther, the Man and His Work*. New York: The Century Co., 1911.

MELANCHTHON, P.: *Corpus Reformatorum*.

MILLER, E. W.: *Wessel Gansfort, Life and Writings*. (2 vols.). New York: G. P. Putnam's Sons, 1917.

MOULE, H. C. G.: "The Epistle of St. Paul to the Romans" in *The Expositor's Bible*. Grand Rapids: Wm. B. Eerdmans Publ. Co., 1943.

MUELLER, E. F. K.: "Predestination" in the *New Schaff-Herzog Encyclopedia of Religious Knowledge*, Vol. IX. Grand Rapids: Baker Book House, 1950.

NEANDER, J. A. W.: *Lectures on the History of Christian Dogmas* (tr. by J. E. Ryland, 2 vols.). London: George Bellard Sons, 1888.

OLSSON, H.: *Calvin och Reformationens Theologi*.

ORIGEN: *Comm. in Ep. ad Rom.*

PERRIN, J. P.: *Hist. des Albigeois and . . . des Vaudois*, Geneve, 1618-19.

POLMAN, A. D. R.: *Predestinations leer van Augustinus, Thomas van Aquino en Calvijn*.

RICHARD, J. W.: *Philip Melanchthon*. New York: G. P. Putnam's Sons, 1902.

SEEBERG, R.: *Textbook of the History of Doctrines* (tr. by C. Hay). Grand Rapids: Baker Book House, 1952.

SNAITH, N.: *The Distinctive Ideas of the Old Testament.* London: Epworth Press, 1944.

STANGE, C.: in *Lutheran Quarterly,* July 1904.

TRAHERON, B.: *Original Letters.*

TYERMAN, L.: *Life and Times of Rev. John Wesley* (3 vols.). 1870-71.

URSINUS, Z.: *Commentary on the Heidelberg Catechism* (tr. by G. W. Williard). Grand Rapids: Wm. B. Eerdmans Publ. Co., 1954.

VAN DEN BOSCH, J. W.: *De ontwikkeling van Bucer's praedestinatiegedachten voor het optreden van Calvijn.*

WARFIELD, B. B.: *Biblical and Theological Studies.* Philadelphia: Presbyterian and Reformed Publ. Co., 1952.

    Calvin and Augustine. Philadelphia: Presbyterian and Reformed Publ. Co., 1956.

    "Predestination" in Hastings' *A Dictionary of the Bible,* Vol. IV.

WEBER, O.: *Karl Barth's Church Dogmatics* (tr. by Arthur C. Cochrane). Philadelphia: The Westminster Press, 1950.

WESLEY, J.: *The Letters of the Rev. John Wesley A. N.,* (ed. by Telford). London: Epworth Press, 1931.

    Works. (32 vols.). Bristol, 1771-74.

ZWINGLI, H.: *Works,* in *Corpus Reformatorum.*